Curacy Express

Curacy Express

A Training Resource for New Clergy

Robert Michael Lewis

WIPF & STOCK · Eugene, Oregon

CURACY EXPRESS
A Training Resource for New Clergy

Copyright © 2016 Robert Michael Lewis. All rights reserved. Except for brief quotations in critical publications or reviews, no part of this book may be reproduced in any manner without prior written permission from the publisher. Write: Permissions, Wipf and Stock Publishers, 199 W. 8th Ave., Suite 3, Eugene, OR 97401.

Wipf & Stock
An Imprint of Wipf and Stock Publishers
199 W. 8th Ave., Suite 3
Eugene, OR 97401

www.wipfandstock.com

PAPERBACK ISBN: 978-1-4982-9529-1
HARDCOVER ISBN: 978-1-4982-9531-4
EBOOK ISBN: 978-1-4982-9530-7

Manufactured in the U.S.A.

The Self Assesment appearing in "Addressing Potential Leadership Flaws" is reproduced with minor changes from *Overcoming the Dark Side of Leadership: How to Become an Effective Leader by Confronting Potential Failures*, by Gary McIntosh and Samuel Rima. Copyright Baker Publishing Group, 2007. Used by permission.

Figure 02, "The Life Cycle of a Congregation," appearing in "Understanding Congregational Life Cycles," is reproduced from *The Life Cycle of a Congregation*, by Martin Saarinen. Washington, DC: Alban Institute, 1986. Used with permission.

Bible quotations are from the New Revised Standard Version Bible, copyright 1989, Division of Christian Education of the National Council of the Churches of Christ in the United States of America. Used by permission. All rights reserved.

To Ellen, without whom none of this work would be possible.

I love you.

Table of Contents

The Covenant-Learning Procedure | ix
Sample Letter of Agreement | xiii

- Leadership 101: What Is a Leader? | 1
- Discovering Your Congregation's Genesis Story | 6
- Understanding Family Systems | 9
- Addressing Potential Leadership Flaws | 12
- Understanding Congregational Life Cycles | 23
- Tribal Christianity | 27
- Does Size Matter? Family, Pastoral, Program, and Resource-Sized Churches | 30
- Boardroom Basics | 39
- Liturgical Environments | 42
- Preparing for Programs | 45
- A Balanced Work Week | 48
- Self-Care for the New Curate | 51
- Small-Group Ministry | 53
- Baptisms from Start to Finish | 56
- Weddings from Start to Finish | 60
- Funerals from Start to Finish | 65
- The Holy Eucharist from Start to Finish | 68
- Healing Ministry from Start to Finish | 70
- Lenten Lessons | 75

Table of Contents

- Hearing Confessions: Counsel and Penance | 77
- The Ecumenical Curate | 80
- Emergence for the Establishment | 82
- Spiritual Direction | 87
- Newcomer Assimilation | 91
- The Catechumenate | 94
- Constructing a Sermon Series | 99
- Using Your Lay Persons to Their Fullest | 101
- Building the Guiding Coalition | 104
- Martyrs, Manipulators, and Mayhem: Dealing with the Problematic Parishioner | 106
- Stewardship Success: Designing a Stewardship Program from the Ground Up | 110
- The Demanding Lover: When Faithful Ministry Becomes an Obstacle to Marriage | 114
- Coping with Crisis: As Local as Your Church and as National as 9/11 | 118
- Moving Out or Moving On: A Pastor Ponders a Change in Ministry Placement | 121
- Quotes from Seasoned Pastors | 125
- Review and Certification | 127

The Covenant-Learning Procedure

THE PROFESSIONAL MINISTRY IN America is undergoing a massive change. It has been said that while many Christians worship in large churches, most churches are small. Fewer and fewer dioceses have the ability to allow for a paid two-year or three-year apprenticeship as in bygone days. The church is changing, and as leaders for the twenty-first century, we must change with the times.

This program represents a fresh idea in clergy training. It is a self-paced resource, which attempts to address the major issues facing the recently ordained seminary graduate. The new clergy person may be in a traditional "curacy" or training program under a seasoned rector in the eastern part of the state. In some other cases, the newly minted curate may find himself called to a mission congregation in the west. For the purposes of this program, the essential training for either of these situations is the same. Here we will address the new pastor as leader and give him or her the tools necessary to be successful.

Structure

This course of training has been designed to be done with a certain measure of accountability. In the following pages, you will find a sample document agreeing to the process. The primary role is that of the "curate" or newly ordained priest or transitional deacon. This is also a partnership, as the whole church has a responsibility to raise up capable leaders. Each curate will have a mentor. The mentor should be a seasoned rector who has many years of successful ministry under his belt. The third player is the diocesan representative. Lastly, the bishop acts as the final authority and

The Covenant-Learning Procedure

judges how well the process worked for each curate. This diocese has particular persons who have interest in overseeing the progress of a new pastor in his or her first ministerial role.

Objectives

You will note that some of the modules contained in this training are geared toward what the new priest does in the congregation. Still many more deal with the new priest as a person. Leadership does not exist simply because a priest is called to fill a position. Leadership is crafted by a person knowing himself or herself, and weaving a tapestry of sorts from past experiences, classroom knowledge, spirituality, independent reading, and learning from failures. There is no perfect leader, but with God's help there can be a pliable leader. That is the one God will use for mighty things.

Journey versus Destination

This training resource is not designed to be completed in a short amount of time. The curate will do well to complete no more than one, or at most two, modules per week. It is essential to examine carefully each module against the backdrop of one's own ministry setting, personal experience, ecclesiastical tradition, and local customs. This is a journey of exploration of the self. Do not cheat yourself by going too fast. Enjoy the journey. You will be learning things that will be beneficial for the life of your ministry, wherever God may plant you in a given season.

Terminology

Every church has its own language. Its leaders are called by different terms. Instead of confounding the reader with a myriad of terms from many settings, this program uses the following terminology:

Board—also properly termed "chapter," "vestry," or "council."

The Covenant-Learning Procedure

Curate—A newly ordained person in his or her first ministry assignment. The term is widely used in Episcopal/Anglican circles. Properly, a curate is a junior-level pastor who has recently graduated from seminary or another school for ministry.

Judicatory representative—Whoever supervises training for ordination or continuing education in a given area.

Mentor—A seasoned cleric with years of experience who offers oversight during the process of *Curacy Express* and commits to a minimum of one hour per week with the curate, either in person or via Skype or Facetime.

Sample Letter of Agreement

Forasmuch as _____(Curate)_____ desires to become a more capable leader and shepherd of the people of God, he commits to the course of formation found in *Curacy Express*. He/she agrees to work diligently and prayerfully over each module and maintain a prayerful attitude. He/she agrees to hear the godly counsel of his mentor and supervisor, inquiring of his/her wisdom and gleaning from his/her experiences.

_____(Judicatory Representative)_____ agrees to shepherd _____(Curate)_____ as diocesan overseer during the course of his study of *Curacy Express*. This person then becomes the final assessor of the curate's progress, culminating in the issuing of the certificate of completion (optional).

_____(Mentor)_____ agrees to serve as mentor. The mentor's role consists of coach, counselor, and spiritual guide, providing insight gleaned from years of experience. He also commits to no less than one hour of individual attention, either in person or by telephone, per week as the curate completes the modules.

Sample Letter of Agreement

This covenant entered into this _____ day of _____, 20____ and attested to by the undersigned:

_____
Curate

_____
Mentor

_____
Judicatory Representative

Leadership 101

WHAT IS A GREAT LEADER?

THERE IS A CONSIDERABLE amount of disagreement as to whether leaders are naturally born or made. I tend to agree with the latter. From my experience, leaders are usually formed out of a crucible of incredibly hard experiences and have a thirst for greatness. The leader is not satisfied with simply existing; he thrives in creating momentum for others to join him on his quest.

More materials are produced on the subject of leadership than nearly any other topic in Christianity, yet still the church is woefully short of leaders. In this unit we will address what a leader is and what he or she is not.

The Leader is a Shepherd

Jesus' own words in John 10:1–42 state the basic needs of church leaders and, in particular, of clergy. The Christian leader is a *shepherd*, uniquely called by God, in a particular place, time, and ministry setting, to guard and care for the sheep. The shepherd had an interest in the sheep he tended. His entire life was traveling out in those fields, so the shepherd had to be quick to defend the sheep from the occasional wolf or bear and also willing to grab the wayward animal back to the flock.

Even though some of the metaphor may be lost on us, as we are not typically living in an agrarian economy, we can still glean the basic premises. God still creates and equips such leaders for our churches. In contrast, the Gospel of John also describes a *hireling*, someone who is in the ministry for the paycheck and the honor, without caring for the lives of each individual sheep. We have many hirelings in our churches and some true, gifted leaders who become so fallen with leadership flaws that they assume the role of hireling when once they were a godly shepherd.

Originally, the labels of shepherd, hireling, and sheep were not meant to be condescending labels. They pointed to a very real function and a promise for the church. Sheep are often seen as dull, simple-minded animals. Their care, even their very survival, depends on the actions of the shepherd. They demonstrate that we leaders, like the sheep, are hopeless without God's shepherding every move of the leader. A sheep that leaves the fold will get into trouble because it needs the wisdom of the shepherd to find green pastures. The church has enough leaders with selfish interests and duplicitous motives. If we are shepherds, we are called to lay down our lives for the sheep, feed them with the truth, and exemplify the reverent submission to God so evident in the ministry of Jesus.

If we fail to have a good relationship with the one we serve, Jesus Christ, our leadership will fail. Often it is easy to get lost in the shepherding and fail to see the Good Shepherd behind it all. As leaders, if we have nothing ourselves, we will have nothing to share. We will all fail and make ministry foibles, but we will rise to the task at hand if we keep our shepherding skills firmly in the grasp of God's tutelage and loving care.

Leadership 101

The Leader Is a Servant

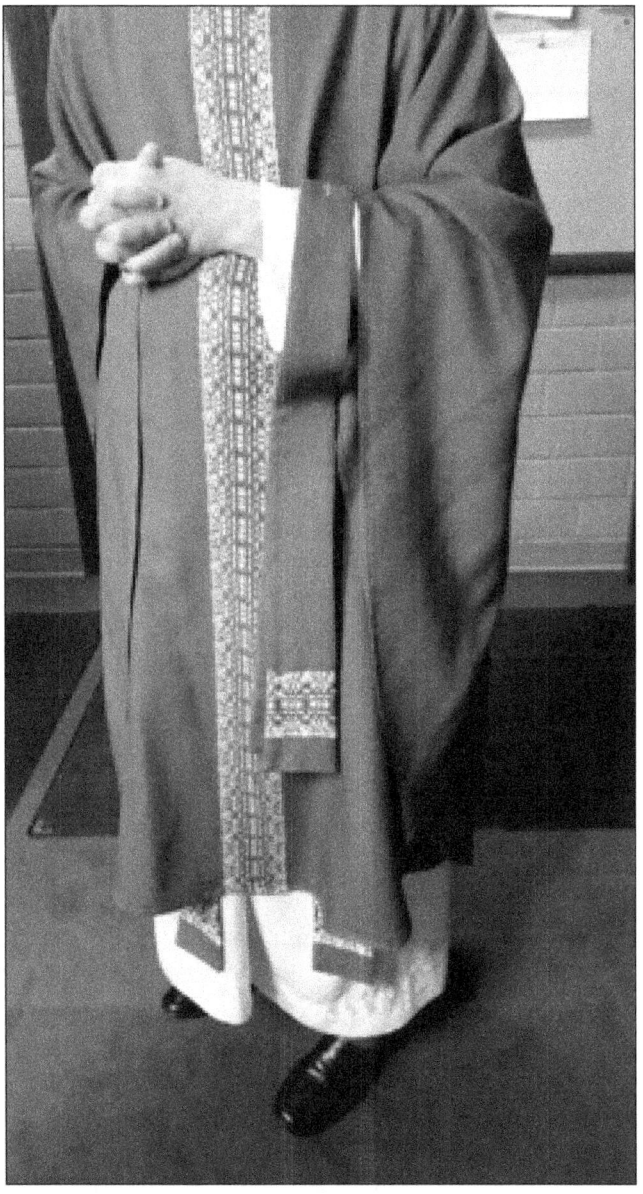

(A priest wearing a maniple over the left arm)

In the Episcopal Church, the church that this author serves, the priests wear vestments. One of the vestments that was traditionally used by priests for well over a millennia is a maniple, a small ornamental towel worn over the left forearm. The prayers that were traditionally said while putting it on evoked the images of the priest's willingness to emulate Jesus by picking up the basin and the towel. In the last thirty years, most clergy no longer wear the maniple. Excuses are that it gets in the way or is embellished beyond its original function. But I counter with precisely the opposite. Our servanthood does get in the way—of serving ourselves. Every time the maniple gets in the way, it reminds us that we are servants first and leaders second. It may be embellished beyond being a simple towel, but that stands as testimony to the royal nature of servanthood. Being a servant shepherd is our calling! Clergy do well to have tangible reminders of that truth.

A true Christian leader who is called by God will always point others to Christ and his church. If they point to the leader, or the passing vanities of the world, the leadership will fail. Our purpose, as Archbishop William Temple said, is to "know Christ and make him known." If your focus is on being a servant and being a shepherd, you will shine as an example of the light that can be found in Jesus.

As you shepherd God's people, you must lead in a proper manner. Your task is to give them hope, energy, a thirst for truth, a life of prayer, and a greater portion of love for Jesus. In all things, your leadership should mirror Jesus' own example. The purpose of the pastor is to align the wills of our people to faithfully and diligently search after God and his truth. You are called to facilitate a true and mature faith, exemplify spiritual maturity, character, love, and trust.

Leaders are not swayed by individual opinions. They stand firm to the resolve the God has given them to do his work and keep to the vision God has provided. Leaders listen to the voice of consensus. In fact, one of the ancient understandings of authority was the *consensus fidelium*, that is, the consensus of the faithful. You will face many challenges and will most certainly fail at some of

Leadership 101

those challenges. That is okay. God is forming in you the character he needs to lead his people. God is forming you to lead and will be forming you for the rest of your life.

You have embarked on a study of leadership. The task of *Curacy Express,* as well as your meetings with your mentor and your report to the diocese, is that you are being prepared as a seasoned leader. As you approach the following units, we will expose some of the "secrets" about leading well.

Questions for Reflection:

- What does it mean to be a leader? To whom do you answer for your leadership?
- Are there things in your daily life and work that may assist you in remembering your call to servant shepherding?
- In your past experience, who was a good leader? Why?
- Were there any bad leaders in your life? What was their legacy?
- People give you permission to lead, and they may revoke that permission. Have you ever known anyone who found that their leadership authority had been taken away because of their inept leadership?
- What does servanthood mean to you?
- What does shepherding mean to you?
- What is a hireling? Have you known any?

For Further Reading:

Brown, Rosalind, and Christopher Cocksworth. *On Being a Priest Today.* Cambridge, MA: Cowley, 2002.

Dulles, Avery. *The Priestly Office: A Theological Reflection.* New York: Paulist, 1997.

Friedman, Edwin H. *A Failure of Nerve: Leadership in the Age of the Quick Fix.* New York: Seabury, 2007.

Discovering Your Congregation's Genesis Story

> "In the beginning when God created the heavens and the earth, the earth was a formless void and darkness covered the face of the deep . . ." (Genesis 1:1–2a NRSV)

THERE WAS A TIME, in the past, when your congregation came into being. Everything was new. Your people rallied around a new mission. Very likely, that was many moons ago. Perhaps a series of leaders has already occupied your post. In some cases, your congregation may be young enough to still have some of the founding families. Still other churches will have been around for a hundred years or longer. Your task in this unit is to explore your congregation's history. In order to understand where you are going, you first need to know where you have been.

In this exercise, you will begin to peruse whatever documents you can find that tell the story of your congregation. Sometimes there are photo albums or even videos of past services. Your congregation is unique—there are no two alike. You are going to discover how very unique it is.

This section is very much what YOU make it. Research the documents, pictures etc. at your disposal and interview some of the "old timers" in your congregation. Let them know what you are doing, and how it will help you understand how best to lead them.

Questions to Ask:

- What were the reasons behind founding this church at the particular place and time that it was founded?

- Who was the first pastor? What was his or her legacy? Did it set the tone for future leaders?
- Most congregations have a favorite pastor in their past. You can use the name to memorialize a former leader while gaining support for an initiative that would have interested that pastor.
- Who is their "favorite pastor" and what was he or she like?
- Has this church ever had a scandal? Has it ever split?
- Has this congregation birthed a "daughter congregation"? If so, when and why?
- What has been the relationship this church has had with the judicatory—amicable or adversarial?
- What have been the successes of this church and where has it failed?
- Describe any major movement(s) where the church grew in average Sunday attendance.
- Did this church ever sponsor candidates for the ordained ministry? If so, who? What was their story?
- When did the church's ministries come into being: examples include women's group(s), men's Bible studies, Vacation Bible School, etc. (You want to pay attention to the gifts of the leaders of these ministries; they will help you understand the traits needed in lay leaders to get things done!)
- What is the social history of the church? Does the congregation host ladies' teas, auctions, or pageants? Does the congregation embrace new ethnicities?

Exercise:

Gather together at least four "old timers" and ministry leaders. Prepare a long piece of butcher paper and tape it to a table. Give each person a different color marker and create a timeline, beginning with the first attempts to found this new congregation and extending well into the future; at the halfway point make a mark to indicate the present.

Be sure to document things that are going on currently in national and world events, the wider church, and the judicatory. They have a bearing on the local church. Lastly, ask those members to plot out their best guess as to the future of the church—KEEP this tool, you will use it for planning as long as you are in your ministry setting.

For Further Reading:

Westing, Harold J. *Create and Celebrate Your Church's Uniqueness.* Grand Rapids, MI: Kregel, 1993.

Understanding Family Systems

ALL TOO OFTEN, PASTORS find themselves called to churches with major underlying issues that persist for generations. Every congregation has issues, because no family is perfect. In this module, we will examine a pivotal issue in understanding the church—family dynamics.

If we examine a healthy church, we see that the pastor exemplifies a "non-anxious presence." Anxiety can be crippling for a congregation simply because it perceives that there is a threat. In the case of a diseased congregation, anxiety may cause certain unhealthy triangles to surface. Have you ever wondered why it is that a seemingly intelligent person who comes out of an abusive family or origin seems to seek out a mate who exemplifies those same issues found in their family of origin? Diseased congregations are no different, simply because all relationships exist within a complex spiderweb of interpersonal relationships. In church life, there simply is no cause and effect relationship. One person never determines change; it is determined by a network of persons.

Case Study: St. Monica's Church

St. Monica's Church is the "problem child" of the judicatory. It seems as though every few years there is a scandal. Let's be clear—nothing criminal has happened. No children were abused. No one ended up in rehab. No money was misappropriated. In every case for the past five pastoral relationships, the pastor has left in disgrace. Many in that diocese refer to St. Monica's as a "pastor-killing" congregation.

The last pastor, a highly energetic, young man, tried many different plans to revitalize the congregation. Each plan was well researched, well implemented, and considered the needs of the surrounding community. After facing multiple obstacles, disheartened, confused, and questioning his own call to the ordained ministry, he resigned.

Reflection Questions:

- Why do you think St. Monica's has this reputation?
- Who is to blame? Can the problem be fixed?
- If you were called to St. Monica's, what would you do to avoid being the next statistic?

Looking Further

St. Monica's was a victim of a diseased system of family triangles. Any attempt to fix the system would be moot if the next leader were not self-differentiated. A leader simply must have the courage to lead even when those around him question his or her vision. In order to get anything done in this type of a situation, the self-differentiated leader needs to be both faithful to his vision and be a non-anxious presence. In many cases, this is precisely what an interim minister does. They come in, maintain a non-anxious presence, and equip a congregation to have a new vision.

In the case of St. Monica's, the pastor repeatedly became the "identified patient." The pastors' work was good, but it did not deal with the underlying disease. Relationships in churches cannot be fixed by identifying the person "at fault." The sad fact is that the whole congregation is "at fault." Sometimes the very best way to deal with such anxiety is to maintain appropriate emotional distance, keep to the vision, and do not succumb to the anxiety when the church is recognizing that the order is changing.

Further Reflection

- Are there any challenges to your vision (or that of the pastor you serve under) for the future of your church?
- Have there been any times in the history of your church when a non-anxious presence was needed? Describe.
- How is it that cause-and-effect thought fails to work in a church? Is any one person ever at fault?
- In your family, was there ever a person who was chronically "at fault"? Could they have been an identified patient?

Terms to Know

Non-anxious presence—A leader who seems unaffected by the stress in an organization. He/she clearly sees the steps needed to enact change.

Identified patient—The person to whom the diseased congregation assigns the blame.

Relational triangles—The fact that in church life, roles are expressed in systems of multiple persons. When one drops out, another fills its place. The roles persist even though the person filling that role may differ.

Appropriate emotional distance—The ability to be so secure in one's leadership that, for the interests of the health of the organization, the leader withdraws from the anxiety. (To be clear, **this is an active role** and is sometimes very costly emotionally for the leader.)

Further Reading:

Friedman, Edwin. *Generation to Generation: Family Process in Church and Synagogue.* New York: Guilford, 1985.
Steinke, Peter L. *Healthy Congregations: A Systems Approach.* Herndon, VA: Alban Institute, 1996.
Martin, Kevin. *5 Keys for Church Leaders: Building a Strong, Vibrant, and Growing Church.* Nashville: Abingdon, 2006.

Addressing Potential Leadership Flaws

EVERY LEADER HAS A weakness. If we simply examine the biblical record, we see a host of leaders with several leadership flaws. Samson was codependent. He needed the affirmation of those of the opposite sex. Jonah was more than stubborn. He was passive aggressive. He knew what God had called him to do, and he actively went in another direction. Moses was a compulsive leader, striking the rock in the wilderness without waiting for God. Saul was a paranoid leader, often fearing that everyone was out to undo his reign. Solomon was a narcissistic leader. He was bigger than life in his own mind. Scripture, as well as life today, is filled with the stories of people with great character flaws.

Every leader has these flaws, in varying amounts and intensities. If we deceive ourselves into thinking that we have none of these flaws, we are missing major spots where God may be willing to transform us into a great leader. Remember, out of brokenness comes healing. Even though there is significant pressure to appear that, as a leader, you have it all together. We also remember that we are broken by nature because we are all redeemed sinners.

Every leader has a past. We are formed by life's experiences. Some effective leaders come from seemingly perfect "Leave It to Beaver" homes. Still others come from a very broken, abusive, and tragic family of origin. Again, Scripture is replete with these examples. The mere fact we all have these character flaws should be of some consolation. But perhaps of even more significance is that the very things that, if gone unchecked, can destroy our ministry, can be the same forces that, if properly channeled, can become great powerhouses of strength in our service to others.

Addressing Potential Leadership Flaws

But before we begin our self-analysis, let's look at an example from recent history:

In the late 1980's, television programs reported with regularity the fall of televangelism's greats—Jim and Tammy Faye Bakker. The Bakkers were a charismatic couple, charming, and by all reports astute businesspersons. Their PTL (Praise the Lord) empire amassed millions, and they had built their next great adventure, a theme park called Heritage USA. This was a theme park built upon Christian values. Reports began to surface about the Bakkers' lavish lifestyle. Some reported that the bathrooms in the Bakker home even had gold-plated faucets. Accountants found the PTL books "troubling." Any doubts about the Bakkers' private life were soon to be confirmed as it was made public that Jim had been involved in a tryst with his aide, Jessica Hahn. As the investigation mounted, it was revealed that the amount of memberships sold to Heritage USA far exceeded their ability to make good of their promises. What caused Jim Bakker's downfall was the evidence that he had taken a cut for himself in excess of three million dollars. Bakker had fallen into one of the great traps for clergy leaders—he had begun to believe himself larger than life. A modern day Solomon, Bakker exemplified the narcissistic leadership flaw taken to its end.

Character Flaws That Lead to Ministry Failures:

- **Pride**—The principal foundation of character flaws that plague ministries
- **Selfishness**—A natural bend toward gratifying one's self
- **Self-deception and wrong motives**—Humans have an intrinsic ability to deceive themselves

Self-Assessment

The following indicator was published by Gary McIntosh and Samuel Rima in *Overcoming the Dark Side of Leadership: How to*

Curacy Express

Become an Effective Leader by Confronting Potential Failures. The exercise will, at first, seem hopeless. It asks you to look carefully and honestly. Remember, this is about redeeming the flaws in leadership. Knowledge is power.

Compulsivity

On the blank lines following each question, score with the following:

1–strongly disagree

2–disagree

3–uncertain

4–agree

5–strongly agree

- I often worry that my superiors do not approve of the quality of my work. _____
- I am highly regimented in my daily personal routines such as exercise schedule or spiritual discipline. _____
- When circumstances dictate that I must interrupt my daily personal routines, I find myself feeling out of sorts and even guilty for having "skipped a day." _____
- I frequently find myself conscious of my status in relationship to others. _____
- It is difficult for me to take an unplanned day off from work responsibilities just to goof around or spend time with family and friends, feeling like a "slacker" if I do. _____
- While away from work, I find myself thinking about work-related topics, often sitting down

Addressing Potential Leadership Flaws

  to write out ideas at length, even if it disrupts family activities. _____

- I like to plan the details of my vacations so I don't waste time or miss anything important. _____

- I often explode in anger after being cut off in traffic or after being irritated by petty issues. _____

- I am meticulous with my personal appearance, keeping shoes shined, clothes carefully pressed, hair carefully cut and groomed, and fingernails clipped. _____

- I frequently comment about the long hours I keep and my heavy workload but am secretly proud of my "work ethic." _____

- When another person makes sloppy errors or pays little attention to detail, I become annoyed and judge him or her. _____

- I am obsessive about the smallest errors, worrying that they will reflect poorly on me. _____

Add the numbers in the blanks. If your total exceeds forty-one, you are likely a compulsive leader. If your total is between twenty-one and forty, it is likely that you have compulsive tendencies. If the total is less than twenty, you probably are not a compulsive leader.

Narcissism

On the blank lines following each question, score with the following:

1–strongly disagree

2–disagree

3–uncertain

4–agree

5–strongly agree

- Fellow leaders in my church or organization frequently question the feasibility of my proposed goals and programs. _____
- I am obsessed with knowing how others feel about my performance. _____
- I find it difficult to receive criticism of any kind. _____
- At times, I find myself fantasizing about how lost they would be if I were not around. _____
- In spite of incredible success in the eyes of others, I find myself dissatisfied and seeking greater things in order to repair my self-esteem. _____
- I am willing to bend the rule and exhibit questionable behavior if it achieves my objectives. _____
- Deep down, I am jealous of the successes of my peers. _____
- I am often unaware or unconcerned about the financial pressures that my plans place on family or my organization. _____
- Success or failure has a direct relationship with my self-image. _____
- I am highly conscious of how those who know me regard my accomplishments. _____
- I need to be recognized or "on top" when meeting with fellow leaders or associates. _____
- I can see myself as a nationally known figure in the future, or have plans to attain such a position. _____

Addressing Potential Leadership Flaws

Add the numbers in the blanks. If your total exceeds forty-one, you are likely a narcissistic leader. If your total is between twenty-one and forty, it is likely that you have narcissistic tendencies. If the total is less than twenty, you probably are not a narcissistic leader.

Paranoia

On the blank lines following each question, score with the following:

1–strongly disagree

2–disagree

3–uncertain

4–agree

5–strongly agree

- When I see key leaders of my organization discreetly talking, I worry that they may be talking about me. _____
- It really bothers me to think that my board or leadership team may meet without my being present. _____
- When an associate receives good remarks about a project or assignment, I experience jealousy rather than the joy of another's success. _____
- I require subordinates or associates to provide me with detailed reports on their work. _____
- I struggle when an associate, rather than me, is asked to take on high-profile activities or tasks. _____
- I have few intimate or meaningful relationships within my church or organization. I find myself avoiding such relationships. _____

- I insist on absolute loyalty from those who work for me and minimize attempts by others to criticize my leadership. _____
- I often worry that there is a growing or significant faction that would like to see me leave the organization. _____
- I have inquired of others about activities of certain leaders in my organization. _____
- Co-workers complain about my lack of a healthy sense of humor. _____
- I refer to those whom I lead as "my people" or "my organization" yet become annoyed if associates make the same remarks. _____
- I tend to take seriously any lighthearted jokes directed at me, feeling that secretly, they may be speaking a seed of truth. _____

Add the numbers in the blanks. If your total exceeds forty-one, you are likely a paranoid leader. If your total is between twenty-one and forty, it is likely that you have paranoid tendencies. If the total is less than twenty, you probably are not a paranoid leader.

Codependency

On the blanks following each question, score with the following:

1–strongly disagree

2–disagree

3–uncertain

4–agree

5–strongly agree

Addressing Potential Leadership Flaws

- I grew up in a family with one or more substance-dependent people (alcoholics, drug addicts, food addicts, etc.). _____
- I grew up in a strict legalistic environment that held its members to a code of moral conduct that was unrealistic and discouraged honest communication. _____
- I am usually willing to tolerate bizarre, embarrassing or inappropriate behavior in others. _____
- I often refrain from sharing my opinion until I have heard the opinions of others in the group—I don't want to stand out. _____
- I frequently worry about the feelings of others, to the point that I do not share my own feelings and risk hurting others. _____
- I often assume responsibility for problems I did not create. _____
- I find it difficult to sleep because I worry about someone else's behavior or problems. _____
- I find myself frequently overcommitted and as though my life is out of control. _____
- I find it extremely difficult to say no to others, even when it will result in difficulty for me or my family. _____
- I consistently feel a sense of guilt but cannot identify the source. _____
- I feel as though I can never measure up. _____
- When others compliment me, I feel compelled to insert some qualifying statement. _____

Add the numbers in the blanks. If your total exceeds forty-one, you are likely a codependent leader. If your total is between twenty-one and forty, it is likely that you have codependent tendencies. If the total is less than twenty, you probably are not a codependent leader.

Passive Aggression

On the blanks following each question, score with the following:
1–strongly disagree
2–disagree
3–uncertain
4–agree
5–strongly agree

- I find myself resisting standards or procedures for formal review of my performance. _____
- It is common for me to procrastinate on major projects I must do. _____
- I regularly resist the ideas of others that could result in a higher workload for me. _____
- I find myself consistently performing beneath my capability. _____
- I experience periodic but regular emotional outbursts, beyond the level that is acceptable. _____
- I intentionally forget suggested projects. _____
- I use the silent treatment to let others know of my anger. _____
- I tell others that everything is "fine" even when I am boiling with anger. _____
- I generally tend to be negative and pessimistic about the future. _____
- Others have expressed that I make them feel uncomfortable. _____

Addressing Potential Leadership Flaws

- Strategic planning and goal setting are difficult for me, thus I resist them. _____
- Sometimes I catch myself trying to manipulate others using anger and emotion to thwart initiatives I oppose. _____

Add the numbers in the blanks. If your total exceeds forty-one, you are likely a passive-aggressive leader. If your total is between twenty-one and forty, it is likely that you have passive-aggressive tendencies. If the total is less than twenty, you probably are not a passive-aggressive leader.

Now you can take plot your scores on the following graph.

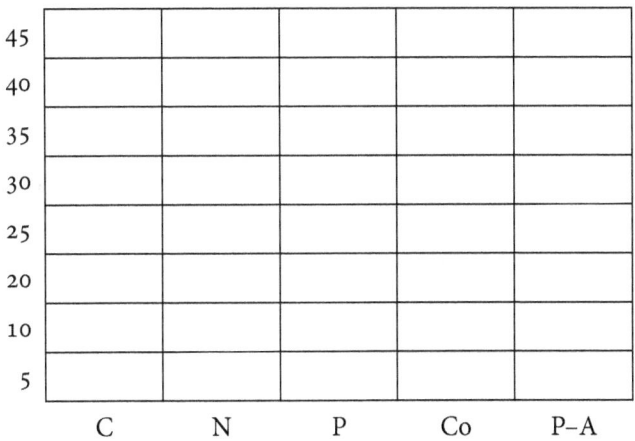

Looking Deeper

We will never completely eliminate our leadership flaws. We are human, and we live in a human world. If we leave our leadership flaw unchecked, however, they can create havoc in our ministry. If we acknowledge the issues and see how our minds work, we can give more and more over to God. When we recognize that he alone is in control of the minutia of our lives, we can be better equipped to cast aside those leadership flaws that could have been our undoing.

Questions for Review

- When you were taking the tests, did you learn anything about yourself? If so, what?
- How does your dominant leadership-style flaw inform how you do your ministry?
- Now that you have become aware of your potential weak spots in your ministry, what safeguards can you take to make sure leadership flaws are changed to leadership successes?
- What issues from your family of origin do you suppose are behind your personality flaws? Do you notice any patterns?

Further Reading

McIntosh, Gary L., and Samuel D. Rima. *Overcoming the Dark Side of Leadership: How to Become an Effective Leader by Confronting Potential Failures.* 2nd ed. Grand Rapids, MI: Baker, 2007.

Understanding Congregational Life Cycles

AT THE TIME OF this writing, most mainline denominations are reporting declining membership trends. The world in which we live is so very different from the one of just a few years ago. In most cases, congregations are oblivious to the slow process of decline. In this unit, we shall examine the natural life cycle of congregations, learn about stages in the birth, life, and death of congregations; and learn a simple strategy for arresting that decay.

When a group of people gets together and decides to start a new house of worship, the energy is intense. There is new vigor and resolve to do the work that God is calling them to do. The birth of a congregation is somewhat of a gamble. Some reports show nearly half of all church plants fail within five years. Usually this is due to internal conflicts and bad leadership. However, if successful, the fledgling congregation often acquires a staff and property. Perhaps most important to realize is the new congregation is forming a history and a DNA—issues we will examine in detail in future units.

If the church plant is successful, the congregation continues to grow. There is great momentum, as what once seemed a dream is now becoming a reality. Usually, around year fifteen or so the church begins to come to a plateau. The membership stabilizes and the congregation is marked by a routine. Many may even describe this as "being in a rut." The plateau stage may seem to last a long time, but the fact is, decline usually begins quickly.

The declining congregation has the most hope if leaders recognize the changes quickly. The longer the church has been in a season of decline, the harder it will be to revitalize it. That revitalization must include a new vision and emphasis. The old dream was realized, and the new dream has to be actively promoted. Revitalization is not for the weak at heart. There may be some opposition, but the leader(s) must be clear about following through.

If the church is unsuccessful at revitalization, it will continue to decline. The plateau usually marks the midpoint in a congregation's life. When there is no longer a collective drive to have a mission, the church enters the death stage. This is not unlike the death stage that we face when we lose a loved one. It is time to remember, to cry over what was lost, and, ultimately, to move on to other places of worship. Sometimes, the death of a congregation can include celebrating that the initial purpose of the congregation has been fulfilled.

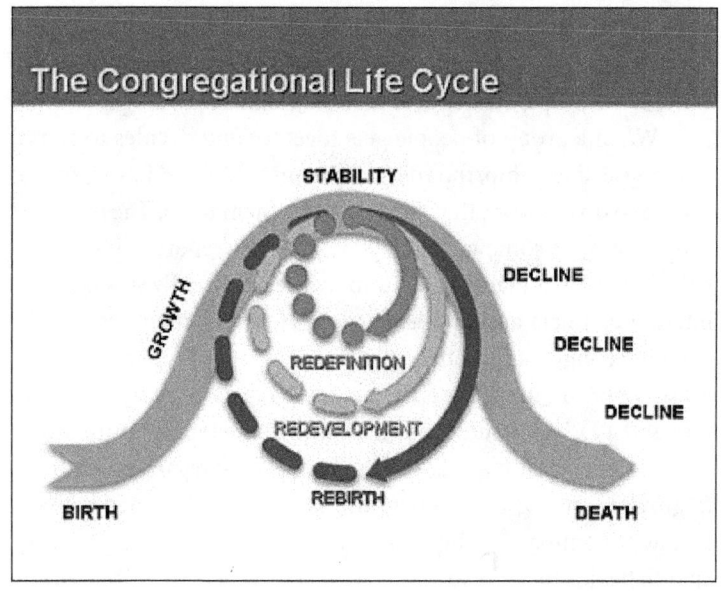

Saarinen, Martin. *The Life Cycle of a Congregation*. Bethesda, MD: Alban Institute, 1986 Used with permission.

Arresting Decay

Think of congregational decay as you would tooth decay. Unless the entire diseased portion of the tooth is removed and stabilized, it will cause surrounding enamel to be plagued until it too decays. Congregational revitalization is not all that different. The decline of an organization is systemic. Here we will analyze how to change decay into growth.

Imagine that your congregation is a living, breathing animal. It feeds on something (God's word and sacraments), it produces something (mission), it breathes (social life), and it excretes waste (deals with problems). The vision of the church is not unlike the circulatory system. Imagine that the heart (the leadership) pumps blood (vision). In due time, the blood changes in structure. Oxygen is replaced by carbon dioxide. The vision of the church accomplishes the work of mission, but if the blood is not re-circulated, it will not keep the organization healthy. New vision is the secret to restoring a declining congregation.

Questions for Reflection:

- What stage is my congregation in currently? How long has it been in that stage?
- Is there a vision? Is it new, or wearied by time?
- Do members understand why visitors stay at this church? Is this a reflection on their true vision?
- Do the buildings and staff fit the vision? Is it understaffed or overstaffed?
- Does the current membership reflect the surrounding area? Is there a demographic group that is over or underrepresented?
- Are members finding their spiritual needs met?
- Are old-time parishioners lamenting the "good old days"? If so, it is probably true that decline has been going on for some time.

- Is your Sunday attendance constant? Are there peaks and valleys when there are no programs or social events at church?

Here is a math problem that will help you understand the attractability of your congregation.

- Easter attendance _____

- Average Sunday attendance _____

Multiply your Easter attendance times 100, divide by your Average Sunday Attendance (ASA).

The answer will tell you how attractive your church is to newcomers and visitors. The higher the percentage is, the more likely that there are new members to be gleaned from the surrounding community. If your attractability number is low (100–130), you may be suffering from "Ghost Town Syndrome." The population may not be great enough in your area to sustain much growth. If your attractability number is high (160–200), questions should be raised as to how well the congregation is doing with advertising, signage and community involvement.

For Further Viewing/Reading

Hansen, Alan. *Waking the Slumbering Church*. Atlanta, GA: Acts 29 Ministries, 2009. (DVD)

Callahan, Kennon L. *Twelve Keys to an Effective Church*. San Francisco, CA: Harper Collins, 1983.

Tribal Christianity

IF YOU ARE A new leader in a church, you are about to find a rude truth. You really have very little power apart from your ordination credentials or academic degrees. Congregations do not function based on immediate authority. They are based on a tribal system.

In normal corporate America, there are forty hours a week in which one gets to know one's co-workers. In relative short order, the workers get to know who can be trusted. Thus relationships are formed with co-workers, and their collective work is strengthened by trust.

Congregations are no different. In order for a new leader to be trusted, rapport needs to be built. That will take time. What you can establish in one week in corporate America requires months of interaction in the church. Remember, they typically only see you for one hour on Sunday, and that is presuming they attend every Sunday, which most churchgoers no longer do.

The remedy for that is in pastoral care. Rapport is established when you baptize new members, bury the deceased, visit the sick, teach the Scriptures, answer questions, hear confessions, and a myriad of other activities that pastors do apart from Sunday services.

Beyond the establishment of rapport is the fostering of certain key relationships. These are the pivotal movers and shakers to which the congregation turns for the voice of authority. Let me be 100% clear, you can have a wonderful decision laid out and adopted by your vestry. If these people say no, it will be perceived as "veto" in the eyes of your people. The larger the congregation, the more difficult it will be to determine who these people are, but every congregation has them and those persons are often quite unaware they hold that role.

Matriarchs and patriarchs are the senior female and male figures in a congregation. They may be past vestry members, in some cases they are retired clergy, but more often than not, they simply are the laypersons that have the most "credited service" within the organization.

One last person to consider in the tribal nature of the church is the storyteller. This is the person with a long and collective memory of the issues, problems, and tales of the past, which season the present and future. These are the folks that stand up at church meetings and say things like, "Remember back in 1960, we were facing the same problem. This was what we did . . . Can we do that now?"

Understanding these pivotal personalities and your own role as the "shaman of the tribe" will help you to understand how best to proceed with leadership. Always remember, make these pivotal persons your allies and you will go far. If you cross them, you can be sure there will be repercussions.

Questions for Reflection:

Who is the matriarch or patriarch of your church? Do you know how she/he became such?

- Have you ever had a disagreement with the "parent figure?" How did that disagreement resolve?
- Looking back over churches you have belonged to in the past, can you identify the parent figures?
- Who is the storyteller in your current congregation? Do you use them as a resource when planning?

Exercise:

Interview the matriarch/patriarch of your church. Consult them about their hopes and dreams for the church. Get a list of some objectives through which they will stand behind you. Make thorough notes. You will use them later when you make strategic plans with your vestry.

For Further Reading:

Pappas, Anthony G., ed. *Inside the Small Church*. Bethesda, MD: Alban Institute, 2002.

Schaller, Lyle E. *The Small Membership Church*. Nashville: Abingdon, 1994.

Does Size Matter?

Family, Pastoral, Program,
and Resource-Sized Churches

The Family Church:
Fifty or Fewer on an Average Sunday

THE SMALL CHURCH CAN be called a family church because it functions like a family. It has parents and children. It is the patriarchs and matriarchs who control the church's functions, even including the leadership. Family churches, I have found, are not so much interested in programming or teaching ministries. They are looking for a leader who is a pastoral presence and conducts a Sunday service that suits their needs. Clergy often make the blunder of thinking that they are the person in charge. In fact, they are the hired hands and the matriarch and/or patriarch is the actual authority. Although it may sound counterproductive, the matriarch or patriarch is primarily concerned that the clergy may take them off on a different direction. Clergy, therefore, are best described as the tribal shaman or chaplain. Some clergy of family-sized churches are of the opinion they are outsiders. Since they are not the hub of the organization, they often fail to understand they are understood that way because all too often, family-sized churches have had a string of incumbent pastors, none of whom stays very long. Thus the leaders with the most credited service are always the matriarch or patriarch. New clergy often make a mistake of having a shootout with the matriarch/patriarch. Make no mistake; such a confrontation will ALWAYS be a losing proposition. The pastor must earn their trust and then use collaborative methods to ensure that the matriarch/patriarch is on board FIRST. If the matriarch/patriarch decides that an idea is bad, the matter is closed. If the priest presses it, it will only discredit him. Avoid taking the parent of the congregation on, even if suggested by other members. To go against the matriarch/patriarch, and ignore that THEY are the authority, is to commit ecclesiastical suicide.

Part of the reason most family churches do not keep clergy for long periods is because they can only pay a part-time salary. In some cases, these congregations are served well by a "yoked" pastorate, whereby clergy are shared between two or more "clusters" of small churches. If clergy accept these positions, it needs to be with the understanding they will need a lot of loving. Many family churches have long lists of former pastors who have used their church as a stepping-stone. It is duplicitous for clergy to accept calls with this in mind, and it does nothing more than engrain the idea that the matriarch or patriarch is truly the one with the best interests of the church at heart.

If you do feel called to such a church, it is important to realize that the more time you give to such a congregation, the more authority you will accrue. Clergy become powerful because they have a long pastorate. The shorter the pastorate is, the more likely that the board is the true authority.

One of the worst places to go right out of seminary—although to do so is becoming a very alarming trend—is to these family churches. You see, seminary graduates are eager to use their seminary education. That works well in pastoral and program churches, but remember, that is not the thrust in the family church. Unfortunately, those same theories are probably very healthy for the church to grow. Unfortunately, because family-sized churches typically are not used to pastors staying long enough to be an effective influence, they are not normally open to new ideas. From my own experience, when a family church does accept new ideas, it builds a certain level of excitement. When the newness wears off, the participation dwindles, and the new pastor begins to take it personally. I have seen some cases where that personal affront is so grand, clergy begin looking for the next ministry opportunity, often repeating the problem with no insight whatsoever in the next family church. If a pastor were interested in breaking the cycle in one of these family churches, it would be wise to plan on staying a minimum of seven years, even if it were necessary to have a part-time secular job as well.

The Pastoral Church: 50–150 on an Average Sunday

Clergy are the center of a pastoral church. There are often a great many parental figures, some of which may have conflicting opinions. Therefore the board and lay leaders look to the pastor as the authority. It is in this situation the pastor needs to learn to build a "guiding coalition," a concept we will address in a later chapter. Such a guiding coalition, if collaborative ministry is possible, becomes the group to which the congregation looks for vision. The power and effectiveness of the guiding coalition depends upon good communication with the congregation and the ability of the pastor to delegate authority where appropriate, assign tasks to be done, and recognize key persons in order to provide a thrust for future accomplishments. If the pastor of a pastoral-sized church does too many things himself or herself or "over-functions," he or she destroys the delicate balance of the guiding coalition, and the leader (probably with compulsive tendencies), burns out very quickly, and his or her guiding coalition feels underused and/or underappreciated.

A key feature of a pastoral church is that lay persons experience having their spiritual needs met through their personal relationship with the pastor. This is why you typically do not have to go through a secretary to see the pastor in such a church. In a pastoral church, it would be rare for any event to meet without the pastor. The pastor's schedule is the church's schedule. The pastor is also reasonably available in times of personal need and crisis. If a parishioner relayed a need for pastoral care, he or she would be seen promptly. This is dramatically different from the family church (where the pastor is often bi-vocational), and the program church (where a secretary would schedule such a meeting with perhaps more time elapsing from call to visit). Being the pastor of a pastoral-sized church can sometimes seem like being stretched like a rubber band. Fortunately, most church members are respectful of the emotional limits of the pastor. A pastoral church often thinks of itself as a family. However, as that family begins to grow, it may make some congregants nervous. Eventually, it will be impossible for the pastor to have special relationships with every member. New people show up and the congregation feels a certain sense of conflict. They know intuitively that a church must grow or die, but they mourn the loss of knowing everyone by name. If clergy do not understand the implications of a congregation exceeding 150, they will quickly burn out and the congregation will shrink back to its former size.

One pastor I knew was well known and loved by his congregation. He was a special friend who had always made establishing relationships of paramount importance. He always made people feel special. Administratively, he was not so gifted, but whatever was lacking in that category was made up for in love. As the congregation neared the 170 mark, he was still running the church in the same way. He was present for everything that happened at the church, and the number of meetings needed quickly exceeded those at which he could be present. The result was disastrous. An up and coming program church began to implode. Ministries gave up trying to get on his schedule, and the pastor quickly admitted he did not know why "his" church was now shrinking. Bottom line—size mattered, and a major opportunity for growth was missed because the pastor had no ability to vary his leadership style.

There are some clergy who function at their highest level of achievement in the pastoral church. The pastoral church often can provide a decent-size compensation package, and most seminaries train their students to be the ideal pastors of pastoral-sized churches. This is the largest sized congregation that most clergy will ever be called to pastor. Going beyond 150 requires great changes in leadership style and gifts, and there just aren't that many large congregations.

Clergy with strong people skills do very well as the pastor of a pastoral-sized church. Such leaders find great reward in being present through the triumphs and tragedies of their congregants. Clergy who enjoy being front and center also do well. Here they can be the primary preacher, leader, liturgist, healer, visitor, and friend. Usually, such leaders are extroverts.

Pastoral personality is key in the pastoral-sized church. People join the church because they like the pastor's energy or charisma. When leadership seems to suffer because the growing congregation has pushed the pastor to the limit, often new helpers will be brought in to assist the pastor in regaining that intimate relationship. Such measures usually fade in short order because the now transitional-sized church needs the pastor to manage a new staff. This means even more administration and less time for pastoral care. Consider the departments held by "transitional" churches: Christian formation, youth ministry, evangelism, stewardship, outreach, and many more. Thus the pastor begins to transition to a far more administrative role as we enter the world of program-sized churches. The transition is costly. Some choose not to make it (like the pastor mentioned previously). Those congregations will hover at about 150, and that will be their permanent threshold. Sacred cows are slaughtered when a pastoral-sized church transitions: easy access to the pastor and the sense of the congregation being a single family are predictable costs of numeric growth.

The Program Church:
150–350 on an average Sunday

The program church meets the needs for a growing congregation to have valuable spiritual care. Whereas a pastor can do such in a smaller setting, now that role falls to programmatic activity. Also the program church is built not simply upon the pastor, but upon small groups. These become mini-guiding coalitions for sub groups or cells in the church. It is nearly impossible to get to this level without small-group ministry. If the church functions well, those cells or ministries are headed by a lay leader who reports to the pastor. If the pastor attempts to fill these roles, it will end up in a type of burnout. That is the pastoral model, not the program model. In good situations, lay leaders also assume some important features pastorally. Perhaps they pray at the meetings for members of their congregation. Teachers and lay leaders often are those who do the "initial intake" that determines there is a pastoral issue about which the pastor needs to be informed.

Clergy are still the hub of the program church, but their role has shifted dramatically. Their time is largely administrative. Planning and maintaining ministries will occupy more time than one-on-one visits. They need to be gifted teachers who can train lay leaders to do different functions well. The pastor is the chief recruiter, actively pursuing new volunteers and heads of smaller ministries. Through all of this, the pastor must ensure that morale is held high and communication remains open. The pastor must invest in the selected few in order for this to work. The Lord Jesus did exactly this with his disciples. He trained them to do the work of ministry, and they reported back to him.

So what can the congregation expect? The pastor will still make hospital calls or emergency visits, but they will probably be very brief. There is not much time for visiting ministry in program churches. The pastor's time is too limited. Such visitation, if possible at all, is far more likely to be done during office hours, and that with a couple of weeks' notice.

If a program church seeks to excel, it must be clear on its mission. Mission statements are helpful, but only if they are quickly memorized. Core values need to be communicated and goals set. Collaborative ministry is essential to maintain this process. In the program church, clergy need to be assertive in defending the goals and values of the church. If concessions are made to individual opinions (as those with codependent flaws may attempt to do), the pastor will be perceived as weak. The program church pastor must be a good assessor of the gifts and skills of lay persons and find the best way to plug them into the church's administrative network.

Clergy who are primarily fulfilled by one-on-one pastoral care would do best to avoid this size church. The amount of administrative work necessary will leave those pastors chronically unfulfilled.

The Resource-Sized Congregation: 350 and Beyond on an Average Sunday

Excellence! If you had one word to describe the resource-sized congregation, it is *excellence*. Since resources abound, these churches provide the highest quality worship experience, programs, outreach and teaching. The pastor of such a church spends far more time preparing sermons and teaching than nearly anything else. The very idea that the church is a family is shattered in these churches. It is impossible to know all the names or even all of the families in a church this size. It is assumed that when the church is called for a pastoral visit, it is the associate pastor who visits, never the rector. Such high quality of liturgy, preaching, and programming comes at the cost of the one-on-one relationship with the senior pastor.

The resource-sized church is defined by a multi-level administration. Harmony among those on the staff is of paramount importance. Without that harmony, the momentum and drive of the staff will suffer. Management of that staff often comes by trial and error. Staffing is best done when a variety of persons have a variety of leadership styles. Momentum is the key. If conflict arises, it must be eliminated.

The pastor who is called to be the rector in a resource church is usually a multi-skilled person who has proven his or her abilities in many pastoral situations. The rector then delegates ministerial and pastoral responsibilities to laypersons and ordained ministers serving under his leadership. By necessity, the rector will need to allow the associate ministers to do their ministry in their own way, and in their own style.

When the multiple staff works well, the harmony of leadership becomes a contagion. Lay people will enjoy the momentum of such a moving organization and will love being part of it. The leaders in a resource congregation need to always be mindful of the momentum. Leadership, by definition, is the ability to create the energy for momentum, not simply assign where that energy is to be used. Creativity and energy is a must for leaders of the resource congregation. If the harmony falls apart, or the momentum runs out of steam, the resource-sized church will begin to decline.

Lyle Schaller, arguably one of the foremost writers on the issue of congregation size and leadership, sums up the congregations as follows: A family church is a cat: it wants you to leave it alone except when it wants to be petted, and it will always land on its feet. A pastoral church is a collie: it always wants to be near the master and experiences anxiety unless the pastor is comforting it. The program church is a farm where the pastor deals with many issues: chickens, pigs, milking cows, and making hay. The resource-sized church is a ranch, and the rancher gets farmhands to take care of all of the many tasks at the ranch, but the rancher keeps all the farmhands in good spirits and working hard.

Questions for Reflection:

- What is the greatest change between the church of 150 and the church of 200 persons?
- Where do you find your congregation? Do the expectations of the pastor's role meet what you expected to be doing with your time?
- In what ways did this teaching challenge your assumptions about how you do ministry?
- Does your understanding of your role as pastor need to be adjusted to "fit" the congregation as they now are?

For Further Reading:

Dudley, Carl S. *Effective Small Churches in the Twenty-first Century.* Nashville, Abingdon, 2003.

Gaede, Beth Ann, ed. *Size Transitions in Congregations*. Bethesda, MD: Alban Institute, 2001.

Martin, Kevin. *The Myth of the 200 Barrier*. Nashville: Abingdon, 2005.

Routhauge, Arlin J. *Parallel Development: A Pathway for Exploring Change and a New Future in Congregational Life*. New York: Episcopal Church Center, 1989.

Schaller, Lyle E. *The Multiple Staff and the Larger Church*. Nashville: Abingdon, 1980.

——— . *Small Congregation, Big Potential*. Nashville: Abingdon, 2003.

Boardroom Basics

ONE OF THE TRADITIONAL tasks for a curate during their term of training is to learn to lead the board. Typically, boards meet either monthly or bi-weekly. Learning to manage your board will be one of your most essential tasks.

Begin with a spiritual exercise. Remember that you need to claim the time for God to work. Consider having each member share the answer to this question: "How have you experienced the working of the Holy Spirit in church lately?" This will allow each member to be heard upfront and minimize the possibility the people will feel unheard. Let each member have their moment. If everyone feels as though their contribution is valued, there will be less chance for ill will or a second meeting forming in the parking lot.

Next, keep to the agenda. Keep in mind that boardrooms are often the laboratories of poorly thought out ideas, so sticking to the agenda is most helpful. Ask (by email or phone) if anyone has agenda items to be considered. If people bring up ideas in vestry, on things not contained in the agenda, it is wise to usually table those discussions so that your people can think about all the logical ends of those decisions.

Keep your board meeting manageable. You are the chair. You determine the discussion. Do not be a tyrant, but subtly and pastorally encourage those who go off on tangents to keep their comments tight and concise. Remember that no one gets saved in a vestry meeting. Address your business and go home.

Dealing with adversarial vestry members can be a real challenge. You will need to develop your own strategy for dealing with such a threat. Usually these persons are not team players and perhaps need to be privately encouraged to find a more suitable ministry than being on the vestry. If you find your vestry divided on an issue, you need to table the vote so a consensus can later be had. If you are short of a concensus by only one "no" vote, or one abstention, you need to assess if it is a good move to pass the measure at that moment. Sometimes it is not a matter of *if* it is wise, but *when* it is wise to pass it.

Financials are a pickle. This author recommends placing them at the end. Usually the financials will dominate a meeting if placed first. The treasurer should be there to back up any questionable entries. A profit and loss (with the budget) statement, checkbook details, trial balance, and balance sheet make up the pivotal financial communications. Unfortunately, most vestry members are not very savvy when it comes to accounting, and most will only look for glaring numbers. Because of this, I usually ask that the financials be approved "pending audit."

A capable secretary or clerk should keep minutes. They should read like a story and not a series of bullet points. They should be posted, once approved, in a public place where interested parties can review them. In most cases, vestry meetings are open meetings. Care should be taken not to ignore guests, but if there are bylaw provisions to include them, do so; welcome them with seat and voice. Normally they are there with a specific purpose.

Chair the meeting and reflect on the following:

- What went according to plan? What was unexpected?
- Were there any surprises?
- If someone attacked an idea, was it done with civility or anger? How do you deal with a board member who is irate?
- Were the minutes approved? Are you satisfied with their content? What could be improved? Were the financials complete? Were there errors?
- Did the meeting stick to the agenda? Were there any members who went on tangents?

- Were there any board members who seemed detached? Can you think of ways to involve them more fully?
- Does anyone in the group attempt to dominate the meeting? Why?
- Did the meeting adjourn at a reasonable hour? (I tend to say that meetings that last for two hours are about one hour too long and filled with one hour's worth of poorly thought out ideas.)
- Did the meeting actually adjourn, or did it reconvene informally in the parking lot? (This is not usually a positive sign.)

For Further Reading:

Michell, Neal O. *Beyond Business as Usual: Vestry Leadership Development.* New York: Church Publishing, 2007.

Webber, Christopher L. *The Vestry Handbook.* Rev. ed. Harrisburg, PA: Morehouse, 2000.

Liturgical Environments

MANY WHO TAKE THIS course may not meet in a stately old church with a traditional pulpit and altar, pews, and organ. For many fledgling congregations, these accouterments are mere dreams at this point. Whether that is your story or you meet in the most established of cathedrals, we will examine together how to create a liturgical environment.

A proper liturgical environment can be modern or Victorian, delicate and intricate or bold and striking. Style is of little value when assessing liturgical environment. It is about creating an atmosphere of prayer.

Case Study: St. Francis Church

St. Francis Church was an old church, built in the carpenter gothic style so popular in the late nineteenth century. It had an impressive carved oak altar, pulpit, lectern, and rood screen. It had some major drawbacks. It was in a neighborhood that was declining. The roof, plumbing, and electrical all needed major improvements. The congregation gathered to discuss the future after the city offered to buy the land in order to expand the adjacent road, and they voted to sell.

Theories abounded as to what should happen next. Would they buy another church, or build one? In a moment of clarity, the patriarch stood up and said, "I think we need to rent a storefront in the middle of the city." That is exactly what they did. They moved the old altar, pulpit, and lectern. The old rood screen was set up not far from the front doors to create a foyer effect and a welcome area. They decided not to move the pews (except for the choir) and purchased modular seating. During the summer, the altar is placed in a circle and surrounded by the people. During the rest of the year, the altar is placed on a platform closer to the far wall.

St. Francis had taken the treasures of the past and made them part of their future. Now they no longer had to worry about their failing building. They simply pay the rent and the custodian of the building takes care of the rest. St. Francis' congregation had discovered that liturgical environments are not tied to bricks and mortar. Liturgy involves using tangible tools for worship with a new and somewhat more flexible setting.

The children of Israel did much the same thing in the wilderness. As the people traveled, the Tabernacle went with them. The furnishings were permanent, but they were simply on the road. An occasional disruption can be a positive thing in the lives of a faith community. When nothing changes for a long period of time, the congregation can grow very wooden in its approach to liturgy.

Case Study 2: The Baptismal Font

St. Bartholomew's Church is the historic gem of the town. It is on the National Register of Historic Places, and many choose St. Bartholomew's as a wedding location, even if they belong to other churches nearby. One lovely feature of St. Bart's is that it has a large, ornate, oak baptismal font, which for generations has stood at the rear of the church in a little niche. In bygone years, the font was only used on Saturday afternoons, as baptism was considered a private affair and usually the precursor to family parties. With liturgical changes in the 1960s and 1970s, the celebration of baptisms moved to Sunday morning. Noting this change, Pastor Jones opted to move (with the board's permission) the font to a central location in the center isle. One month later, one of the young ladies of the congregation announced her engagement and plans were underway. Her mother asked about the possibility of moving the font back to its former location. The pastor refused and tempers flared. Rightfully, he did not want one wedding to dictate the usage of liturgical space. The mother did a great deal of talking to people in the congregation about this issue and tried to raise some support among the congregants. Thankfully, the voice of reason prevailed and the matriarch of the parish, who was on the altar guild, offered a compromise to both Pastor Jones and the mother of the bride. The font would be moved below the pulpit and decorated with flowers especially for the wedding.

Questions for Reflection:

- Why do you think people are reluctant to change their worship setting?
- How do you define sacred space?
- What sights, sounds, feelings, etc. do you associate with worship?
- What makes an area prayerful?
- What are the sacred cows? Every congregation has things they are unwilling to even temporarily alter. What are they?

Exercise:

- Set up an alternative worship experience. Use items that are associated with worship in traditional spaces. Create a mood conducive for worship. Arrange chairs in different ways (in a circle, or with rows facing in toward the center isle).
- Conduct your worship service and poll a few people. How did it feel? Did you feel close to God?

For Further Reading:

Zimmerman, Joyce Ann. *The Ministry of Liturgical Environment.* Collegeville, MN: Liturgical, 2004.

Preparing for Programs

ONE OF THE MOST exciting things that a pastor of a church will do is to develop a programmatic life for his or her congregation. It is a time when the congregation's dreams of a stronger church can be realized, and it also can be a time of immense frustration. In this unit, we will address one of the major issues that causes church programs to fail and how to positively direct programmatic activity for the best growth.

"Old Timers"	"Allies"
Older than pastor, part of church before pastor's arrival	Older than pastor, came to church as a result of pastor's ministry
"Families"	"Consumers"
Younger than pastor, part of church before pastor's arrival	Younger than pastor, at church because of services provided

The chart above illustrates four groups of people you currently serve. Every parish typically has a representation of each. Understanding each group will help you make programmatic decisions for your church. Failing to understand them may lead to some very unsuccessful programs.

The "Old Timers" are the matriarch and patriarch, the storyteller, and those with the most steady attendance. They typically have the largest pledges and are invested. They were there before you arrived, and they will be there after you leave for another ministry calling. People in this group, although not interested in programs themselves, are acutely interested in the health of the church. You will need their consent and help to get your programming off the ground. They are also acutely interested in the well-being of the "Families" because they are often their children or grandchildren.

"Allies" are those who are drawn to the church because of your style of leadership. They may like the liturgy or preaching you provide. They also are one of the better places to invest in programmatic activity. They are there because you offer what their souls crave. You have a unique ability to reach them where they are, and they have a vested interest in having you as their pastor, often even more than any other group in the church.

"Families" are often fickle because of their age and because of the distractions of post-modern life. Their Sunday attendance may be spotty, but is often grounded because their parents may be "Old Timers." They understand this as "their" church, and this may be the only church they have ever attended. If you build programs for them or their families, you will solidify their commitments.

"Consumers" are those young families who come to church based on what services you provide. They typically are very hesitant to commit to anything and are present because the church offers things that are free. They are interested in what the church provides, and when it fails to provide it, they move elsewhere. They are as perennial as the grass in terms of building a church. If you place your programmatic thrust here, it will not have staying power.

"Making Lasagna"

In my first ministry setting, I offered a program called "Bringing up Boys," by the publishing house Focus On The Family. I made a great deal of preparation. I had a radio ad on the local top forty station, put signs in every laundromat, grocery store, day care, and school. Each flyer had a tear-off section with the church's phone number, address, time and date. It also noted dinner would be provided and the meal and program were free.

Preparing for Programs

About a month passed and the date drew near. I drove around town and was greatly encouraged. Almost all of my tear-off tabs were gone. I prepared lasagna and had everything ready. That night, I got a call of encouragement from the bishop, saying, "Let me know how it goes. We would like to try this in some other places in the diocese." The time for the event came—and went. Fifteen minutes later one person drove up, walked into the parish hall, and then asked if this was an AA meeting. I was devastated. Hours of prep work and cooking and all was for nothing. Our family would eat leftover lasagna for what would seem like forever.

I called the bishop the next day and lamented. He gave me some excellent advice I have treasured: "Robert, no attempt at ministry is ever a failure. God will use this preparation at another time in your ministry when you would not have the time to prepare so well. Always remember, we are called to faithfulness, not success. The success is God's." This was a great learning experience for me. Don't direct your programs to "Consumers"—it rarely works out.

Exercise:

Plan a one-day retreat. Make or adapt a program that would be of interest to the community and to the parish. "Parenting with a Christian Perspective" or "Finances God's Way" may be good themes. Take the lead from your "Old Timers." What programs would they like to see?

Review the results with your mentor. How well did the program work? Who came? Curious "Old Timers"? "Families"? "Allies"? "Consumers? Do you think the program bore fruit? Did you "make lasagna"?

A Balanced Work Week

THOSE OF YOU WHO have previously identified yourselves as having either compulsive or passive aggressive dominant tendencies may have trouble with this exercise. Here we will look at the power of balance in all facets of the pastor's life. It is natural to want quality free time and a productive workweek. But how do we attain balance in such a way that our priorities remain intact?

I have often marveled at the outline of St. Paul's letter to the Ephesians. It seems to be a model for the balanced leader's life. St. Paul addresses our priorities in this order, and I hold that this is not an arbitrary arrangement: God first, spouse second, children third, work fourth, ministry fifth. For the pastor, ministry is joined to our work, but not necessarily joined to our first allegiance. Often the pastor becomes more worried about the spirituality of those in his or her charge to the point that their own personal prayer life suffers. Corporate spirituality does not replace individual devotion. Praying with others does not replace quiet time with God.

Spouse and children need to have special times carved out or they will begin to resent both the pastor and the congregation. They give up much to be part of a pastor's household and continually have to share their loved one with the larger community. Be very careful to schedule time with them. Ministry can be a demanding mistress, so guard your marriage against the perils of ministry overload (more about that in a later session).

One way that I have found is helpful in planning my workweek has been to divide my week into twenty-one units. You do not count your sleeping hours. You divide your waking hours into three equal segments: morning, afternoon and evening. During the week, twelve units belong to the ministry, six units belong to

A Balanced Work Week

your family and three units are your personal Sabbath. When I say personal Sabbath, I am not referring to the day you get all of your errands done. Spend time in rest and refreshment. Enjoy your family and give thanks during that twenty-four hour period.

Why units? Simply said the stresses of ministry are such that you will need to shift your schedule often. Emergencies come up in the life of the church and you will need to allot time to them. Personal issues will also sometimes need to come during the typical working hours. Be flexible. Share your plan with your family and office help. Make them understand you need a balanced workweek.

Exercise:

Please do not skip these steps but do them, all in the order of the letter to the Ephesians.

- Plot your typical workweek on a desk calendar.
- Divide all seven days in thirds.
- Which day (three blocks, uninterrupted) is your **personal Sabbath**. Color it blue. (Blue is for rest and refreshment).
- Which six blocks of time should be **reserved for your family?** Color them yellow. (Yellow is for caution, lose these and your family time will suffer).
- Which twelve blocks are for **ministry**? Color them red (the first liturgical color of the church).

Questions for Reflection:

- Was this exercise difficult? Did it challenge your perceptions of time and priorities?
- What is your greatest scheduling challenge? Why is it important to deal with that problem?

- If you are married (and/or have a family), share this exercise with them. What are their opinions of it? Will they hold you accountable to this plan?

For Further Reading:

Muck, Terry. *Liberating the Leader's Prayer Life.* Waco, TX: Word, 1985.

Self-Care for the New Curate

MINISTRY IS EXCITING. It is also draining. You will see people at their best and also at their spiritual low points. You will celebrate the sacraments of the church. You will also be called into action when God's children behave badly. When children rebel, you will be consulted. When marriages are in jeopardy, you will be called. When matters of life and death arise, you will be the one who your people trust for the word from the Lord.

It would be foolhardy to think you can do this on your own power. A personal plan is necessary to help you unwind from the stresses of ministry. If you have no plan, the crises will arise and you will have no way to deal with them. In these cases, pastors may result to artificial means to numb themselves from the stresses of ministry: drugs, alcohol, isolation, even inappropriate relationships. A pastor is not an island; he or she is part of the body of Christ. To minister effectively is to know how to minister to self.

Reflection Questions:

- What helps you unwind after a hard day at the office? Is it constructive?
- What stresses of ministry prove challenging to you?
- Do you find yourself drawn to maladaptive ways of coping with stress? If so, what? What do you think can replace it?
- Are your spouse or children supportive of your self-care? If not, have you explained the need to care for self?

Mentor Time:

Ask your mentor to share his or her tips for self-care. How does he or she decompress? Has this ever been a challenge?

For Further Reading:

London, H. B., and N. B. Wiseman. *Pastors At Risk: Help for Pastors, Hope for the Church*. Wheaton, IL: Victor Books, 1993.
———. *Your Pastor is an Endangered Species*. Wheaton, IL: Victor, 1996.

Small-Group Ministry

ONE OF THE CHALLENGES of any congregation is fostering relationships and spiritual growth. These things simply cannot be achieved overnight, so this unit will focus on a mindset. Research has proven those churches that have small groups as the core of their common life tend to be closer, more spiritually enriched, better stewards, and tend to be growing. For many churches, however, the last sixty years or so has done much to enforce the idea of church as a quasi "country club." People come for a service and then depart until the next meeting the following week. They drop their "dues" in the plate, but may have little to do with the church during the week. This is a recipe for a dying church, and it is pandemic in the United States.

One tactic (if the church is newly planted) is to have membership in a small group mandatory for membership. Yes, sometimes membership that is more personally costly has more of a value to the congregation. There is no one-size-fits-all strategy to small groups. Some small groups center around reading or a particular craft. Don't forget it is helpful for the church to have groups that, although not necessarily doing spiritual things, are nonetheless sharing with spiritual people. Below is a list (but by no means exhaustive) of potential small groups:

- Men's Community Service
- Softball
- Needlepoint
- Promise Keepers
- Young Mothers

- Young Fathers
- Single Parents
- Caregivers Support Group
- Recovery Groups
- Empty Nesters
- Gen X, Y, Z
- Bowling League
- Singles Group
- Gardening Club
- Creation Care Group
- Women's or Men's Bible Study
- Fellowship (or Hospitality) Group

. . . and many more

Each congregation has a fingerprint of sorts. The small groups should reflect the uniqueness of that community, its gifts and strengths, as well as the way its members believe God is calling them to shape their neighborhoods and communities.

Although it will have a predictable cost, a new pastor may either insist or strongly encourage new (or even existing members) to be part of a small group. Remember, this is about discipleship. God wants us to have a close-knit system of relationships, and when that is in place the congregation as a whole will be a more united front.

Questions for Reflection:

- What small groups already exist in your ministry setting?
- Can you envision the birth of a new group or groups based on the current membership?
- Are there old groups that need a bit of encouragement?

- What is the legacy of small groups in your ministry setting?

Mentor Time:

Ask your mentor about his or her experience with small groups. What worked? What failed? What small groups are working in those churches right now?

For Further Reading:

Arnold, Jeffrey. *The Big Book on Small Groups.* Downers Grove, IL: InterVarsity, 2004.

Donahue, Bill, and Russ Robinson. *The Seven Deadly Sins of Small Group Ministry: A Troubleshooting Guide for Church Leaders.* Grand Rapids, MI: Zondervan, 2002.

Baptisms from Start to Finish

BAPTISM IS A CELEBRATION of new life. It is a pivotal point in which a life is united to Jesus Christ in his death and raised into his resurrection. It is also a community event, and it reminds us all of our own baptism and the promises that we made or that were made for us on our behalf.

Baptism is also a service rich in symbolism. There are many factors or traditions that can be included, which will be explained later. As part of your crafting of a rich baptismal service, you might consider which ones may be useful in your ministry setting.

First, let us examine the setting for baptism. Perhaps it is a font or an open baptistery. In the early church, baptisms were done with cold running water. The candidate would feel "death" from being plunged into icy waters. While that may sound novel for adults, it is ghastly for children. In this case, warm water is a must. You might also consider using a nearby lake, stream, or ocean. It does not really matter if the water is salt or fresh.

Another consideration is the age and agility of your candidate. Holding a baby over a font is easy. However immersing a ninety year old with severe osteoporosis is quite another matter. Ideally, symbols, like water, should be large enough to be seen by the congregation. The more water, the richer experience for all. A gentle sprinkle is not very enriching for the congregation as a whole.

Look at the following list. Which of these traditions would be appropriate in your ministry setting?

- *Amount of water*—In some settings the font is large enough to immerse infants, but only to pour on adults. If at all possible, avoid sprinkling. The more water used, the more the congregation can visually participate in the action.

- *The use of candlelight*—Most churches use a "paschal candle," symbolizing the resurrection. In some churches the paschal candle is even dipped into the font as the waters are being blessed. Still other churches present a lighted candle to the newly baptized or to the sponsors. If held at night, the flickering of the individual candles adds to the special feeling of the experience. Consider a vigil service on Easter Eve, the Eve of Pentecost or the evening before the Sunday after All Saints' Day.

- *The use of oils*—Traditionally two types of oils have been used in conjunction with baptism. One, called Oil of Catechumen, is scented like lemons (or unscented) and is administered after the candidate renounces Satan and all the spiritual forces that rebel against God, but before the candidate receives the water of baptism. Often, it is used in private, before the service starts. The second oil, called Chrism and scented with myrrh, is applied after baptism and symbolizes the permanence of the sacrament and the presence of the Holy Spirit in the newly baptized person.

- *The use of salt*—Many times the baptism of an infant is accompanied by the salt of wisdom. This salt is blessed that the candidate would receive spiritual wisdom and discerning in their earthly pilgrimage. A few grains are administered by mouth either without words or by saying something to the effect, "Jesus said, 'You are the salt of the world,' therefore be salt and light to this hurt and broken world."

- *The sprinkling of the people*—Using a bucket and a branch or aspergillum, sprinkle the gathered community as a reminder of their baptism.

While all of the added features add to the meaning of baptism, essentially the water is the only element. Choose carefully if there are existing traditions in your ministry setting and after careful planning with the candidate or family.

Every baptismal service should be preceded by some manner of instruction. In some settings, a longer period of instruction called "the catechumenate" prepares adult converts for the sacrament. Still in other churches, such preparation is reserved for confirmation. The Acts of the Apostles make clear a certain order of events; simply, the person repented and was baptized. It was only when the church discerned the need to weed out spies from among the catechumens that the practice of preparation became longer (in some cases as long as three years). Choose carefully how you wish to prepare your people for the sacrament. You do not want to forego instruction, but it is not wise to make getting baptized too difficult either. Some churches offer what has been called "open font." This is an opportunity for anyone to be baptized at a service geared for seekers who wish to be part of a Christian community. You must judge, in consultation with the judicatory, what is the proper procedure in your ministry setting.

Questions for Reflection:

- What means of preparing the candidates (or their families) would you employ?
- Is there a tradition in your ministry setting of how and where baptisms are to be celebrated? Describe.
- Would any of the added symbols appeal to you? Would they work in your ministry setting?
- Why is it important to have baptism as a public rather than private sacrament?
- Reflecting on your own baptism or those of your children, what baptismal traditions are important to you? Why?

Exercise:

Plan and conduct a baptismal service. Describe with your mentor the steps you took, both in pre-baptismal formation and the liturgical resources you used. Describe the symbolism and the setting. After completion, how did it go? Would you change anything next time?

For Further Reading:

Ferguson, Everett. *Baptism in the Early Church: History, Theology, and Liturgy in the First Five Centuries.* Grand Rapids, MI: Eerdmans, 200.

Weddings from Start to Finish

WEDDINGS ARE A TIME of feasting, joy, and family. They can also be a time of unrelenting stress. I have always said it was far easier to do a funeral than a wedding. The bar of expectations is very high. The liturgy has to be perfect—if there is such a thing as a perfect service.

Before we deal with the service, let us deal with the pastoral issues surrounding marriage. Whatever marriage preparation you are doing, be sure to stress the spiritual issues surrounding this lifelong union. Check with the judicatory if one or both of the parties has been married before and the former spouse is still living. You may need permission and a written marital judgment for something like that to take place.

Questions to Ask along the Way:

- Where will this couple be living? Are they living together now?
- How long has this couple known each other?
- If this marriage involves children, what are their opinions about their potential step-parent?
- Are both persons willing to commit to attending your church regularly? If not, you will need to decide if you wish to preside at the marriage.
- Has the couple spoken freely about issues of sexuality, family planning, and what that means in a marriage?

- If either party has been married and divorced, have they had the appropriate therapy? (Remember, there is no one party that is to blame for the breakup of a marriage—we exist in relational triangles.)
- How does the couple define love? Can they define it? Is it a feeling or a decision?
- Have both parties completely disclosed their finances, including debts and loans?
- Inquire about each partner's family of origin. How does this inform their thoughts about marriage?
- Do they understand that marriage is lifelong, a sacred commitment, and that their vows are to God and their spouse until death? (Note: the existence of a prenuptial agreement indicates that there is not sufficient intent to go through with a marriage.)

The Wedding Ceremony

Now we get to the brass tacks of planning a service. While many brides have had long-standing ideas about what they want in their service, now is the time to be clear—you are the final word. Not the couple, not the mother of the bride, not the photographer! It will help you to set down some ground rules. While each cleric will need to develop his/her own, here are my guidelines, and I share them hoping they will help you:

- On the day of the wedding, if I detect that any of the marriage party is under the influence of any mind-altering substance, alcohol, or drugs, the wedding is off—PERIOD. You cannot expect people to fully consent if they are inebriated.
- The music is chosen with the consultation of the church musician. If he or she says no, then the answer is no. Any additional musicians must be approved by the church musician.

- A celebrant from a different church or tradition is permitted only if I am in agreement.

- Photographers may take flash photography only before or after the service. Pictures or video taken during the service must use only the ambient light in the room.

- I reserve the right to dictate where flowers may be placed, and certainly NOT on the altar mensa (tabletop).

Case Study: St. Thomas

Cassandra's wedding was quite the production. There were six bridesmaids and six groomsmen. It was an afternoon affair in early June. Nearly three hundred people were in attendance. The choir had been paid to do a special anthem. A string ensemble played the prelude. A reception was planned at the local yacht club. The mayor and city planner were in attendance. This was a very big deal indeed!

The mother of the bride was a fastidious woman. Every detail of the wedding she obsessively controlled. Most frightening was the constant coaching she gave to the bride. It was quite obvious that this was HER affair and not the bride's.

The wedding began. Organ fanfare accompanied strings, the bell carillon sounded, and the procession began. The bridesmaids and their groomsmen processed and then the organ modulated to a new piece for the bridal procession. Cassandra appeared in her dress, escorted by her very proud father. Midway up the aisle, overcome by the planning and anxiety, and amidst the pressures of the moment, she vomited all over herself.

Her father took her quickly into the sacristy, and the attendants helped clean her. She changed into one of the bridesmaids dresses and then had one of the more beautiful and meaningful weddings. The air of perfection was gone. It could never be achieved. The business of marriage was achieved, even though the "show" was now over.

Questions:

- How would you have handled Cassandra's wedding differently? Could you have avoided the mishap?
- What is the appropriate role of the mother of the bride?
- How much "show" is just too much?
- Did Cassandra's wedding illustrate something wrong about North American weddings? What is wrong? How can clergy fix it?

Planning the Wedding

Exercise:

Plan a wedding or a renewal of marriage vows. Follow the outline below. Reflect often with your mentor on the process:

- Complete a period of pre-marital counseling with your couple.
- Set a date for the wedding (you will need a minimum of four months to plan. If there is a reception other than in the fellowship hall, you will need a year!)
- Discuss what the liturgy will look like (use your tradition's resources). Discuss things like participants, choreography, and symbols.
- Discuss vows. If you allow your couple to write their own vows, make sure that they are not emotion-laden drivel. They should state a decision is being made and the decision is lifelong.
- Talk about music. What music genre will be used? If outside of sacred repertoire, be careful. The tune "Here Comes the Bride" comes from Wagner's opera, *Lohengrin*. The wedding in that opera deals with dark subject matter like paganism, possible infidelity, and tragic death. It is probably best to stick to the classics.

- Will the celebration include Holy Communion? If you are inviting your guests to a banquet after the wedding, should it not include an invitation to the table of the Lord?
- Talk about the church community. Help the couple to realize this is a day not simply in their life, but in the life of the community. Help them realize that their church community is an essential part of their marriage. Stay close to the church, and the marriage will be better.

Mentor Time:

Discuss with your mentor what weddings in his or her history have gone well. What could have been better?

For Further Reading:

Covino, Paul, ed. *Celebrating Marriage Preparing the Wedding Liturgy: A Workbook for the Engaged Couple.* Rev. ed. Portland, OR: Pastoral, 1998.

Funerals from Start to Finish

OF ALL THE TIMES a cleric is invited into the life of his or her parishioners, the time of death is most sacred. We are a resurrection people. We speak of life everlasting, and our actions should all point to that fact. During this module we will examine the issues surrounding death: counseling, funerals, and aftercare.

Notification of Death

Whenever a member of the church dies, a visit from the pastor is in order. It is a time not simply to be there for the family, but also to offer the appropriate prayers for the deceased and to follow your tradition's protocol for ministration at the time of death.

Often, the death of a parishioner will feel personal. They are part of your family, and it is ok to feel the loss. Remember that Jesus wept at the grave of his friend Lazarus before he raised him to life again. Honor your own grief. If you grieve, the family will understand, and it will make you far more approachable. They will know that you loved the deceased. Be sure you notify the church members.

Planning the Funeral

Much like weddings, there is now an attempt (largely driven by the funeral home industry) to over-personalize a funeral. While a certain amount of personalization is acceptable, guard yourself from diluting the real purpose. The purpose of the funeral is twofold:

- Proclaim the gospel
- Commend the deceased to God

It is entirely appropriate to memorialize the deceased provided you do not lose sight of the fact that this is a liturgy. The life of the deceased should be a testimony in word and example to the God he or she knew and loved. Keep in mind that the appropriate place to commend the deceased to God's mercy is in church and not in a funeral home. Funeral homes deal with the reality of death. The church deals with the reality of everlasting life.

Exercise:

Meet with the family of the deceased and plan the service using the following guidelines:

- Where will the services be held?
- What will the service look like? Communion?
- What lessons from Scripture will be read?
- Would someone like to give a witness? (best placed right after the opening prayer, before emotion sets in.)
- Plan your sermon.
- Plan a reception with the family. Who will provide food—church ladies or a catering firm?
- Where will the body be interred? Will the body be buried in a casket or cremated?

After the funeral, make an appointment to speak with your mentor. How did the funeral go? Were there any things that you would do differently? Take time to talk about funerals with your mentor, it is one of the most important services you provide to your people.

Aftercare

The worst part of mourning is often two weeks to one month after the loss of a loved one. It is during this time that the cards cease coming and the flowers have all wilted and died. Then the grim reality of the silence left by the departure of the loved one becomes crystal clear. In Kübler-Ross language, the mourner enters the phase called acceptance. A courteous and caring pastor will go out of his or her way to provide contact with the surviving family during these times.

Exercise:

Make it a point to visit the family of the deceased in the period between two weeks and one month after the passing. Pray with them and offer comfort. Share your experience with your mentor.

For Further Reading:

Bane, J. Donald, et al., eds. *Death and Ministry: Pastoral Care of the Dying and Bereaved.* New York: Seabury, 1975.

The Holy Eucharist from Start to Finish

OF ALL OF THE things we do routinely as pastors, the celebration of the Holy Eucharist is our greatest joy and privilege. I was fortunate to have attended a seminary where they walked you through every step of this process before graduation, but these days more and more priests will have had non-traditional ordination tracks and will likely not have had the same in-depth liturgical training.

You will come to the altar with your own preferences. You will appreciate high church, low church, or broad church traditions. The vast majority of the churches in my tradition would be considered broad. You will be asked to lead a church with a great deal of their own traditions. Some of them will be rather longstanding. If you choose to change something, do so only with thorough education, patience, expectation of some level of resistance. I would also advise that you make such changes in the first few weeks of your tenure. In this way you use the "honeymoon period" to your advantage, and can claim some level of ignorance to your advantage. If you wait, you will have a harder time with any liturgical changes.

There is a wealth of liturgical resources available in our tradition and I commend four of them to you. However, you need to know they have their own biases, and I have found it is best to use a little of all of them. Listed below are some that my tradition utilizes:

For Further Reading:

Lamburn, Edward. *Ritual Notes: A Comprehensive Guide to the Rites and Ceremonies of the Book of Common Prayer of the English Church*. London: Knott & Son, 1956.

Dearmer, Percy. *The Parson's Handbook*. London: Grant Richards, 1899.

Galley, Howard E. *Ceremonies of the Eucharist: A Guide to Celebration*. Boston: Cowley, 1989.

Mishno, Dennis G. *A Priest's Handbook: The Ceremonies of the Church*. 3rd ed. New York: Morehouse, 1998.

Set the Stage:

Your Altar Guild will have a history. Unless you interject with new instructions, the assumption will be that you will conduct your services in the same manner as your predecessor. Take time to meet with your Altar Guild to discuss colors, special celebrations, and your preferences. Remember, you have the final word on the manner and customs of worship, but if you pull rank more than once, it will undermine your leadership.

Exercise:

Using your Sunday bulletin, note what changes you think would be appropriate in your ministry setting. Answer the following questions:

- What precipitates this change? Is it for pastoral reasons?
- What type of education needs to surround your liturgical change?
- Can this change be considered a "recovery" of something old?
- Are you prepared for backlash?

Talk over these concerns with your mentor. Glean his or her wisdom from their past changes. Ask your mentor about any bad changes they had done. Would they have changed the way they went about that change. Be careful to listen to their wisdom, it will save you your own pain.

Healing Ministry from Start to Finish

THE MINISTRY OF CHRISTIAN healing is one of the most powerful pastoral functions of your office. When you are called into times of great stress, your presence itself will be healing. In this unit, we will examine the steps needed to create a healing ministry in the local church. Try to remember, there are wonderful laypersons in your congregation who have the gift of healing as well. Share this ministry with them.

Seventy-three percent of the recorded actions of Jesus in the gospels are moments of healing. As a pastor, you will be called into settings where it will be expected you will provide a similar ministry. Remember that in your ordination, you were given whatever spiritual gifts were necessary for your ministry—that includes healing.

But in this module, we will take it a step further. Some curates will be in churches with well-established programs such as the Order of St. Luke, and still other parishes will have a very dysfunctional understanding of healing. It will be your challenge in this unit to examine what is working, what is not working, and what must change for the health of the church.

History records that the church has had a varied response to the ministry of healing. At times, it was suppressed, clericalized, or usurped by the monarch. In the early church described in the New Testament, healings were commonplace. Part of the fuel for the evangelism seen in the Acts of the Apostles was due to Christian healing. We see works of everyday miracles in the lives of ordinary Christians. I understand this is the ideal for today. We are entering into a time when we will need to return to the roots of our New Testament heritage. The church is not the establishment anymore.

Curiously, when we look at history, and particularly the New Testament, we see that the ministry of healing was always the precursor to evangelism. Sadly, this was lost in time, to the point that many even believed that the "Age of the Apostles" included supernatural healing but not the modern day. Such assertions are, of course, preposterous when we hold to the clear teachings of Jesus, that we would be known by these works.

Historically, the church began to restrict works of healing so that they became officially the work of priests only. Miracles became somewhat few, and the church relegated the sacrament of Anointing of the Sick or Holy Unction only to times when the patient was in fear of death. One reformer even attacked the practice of last rites saying that it would be preferable for the oil to be used on people with the capacity for life, instead of the "half-dead." The reformer was, of course, right. The sacrament is for the restoration of the living, not simply the comfort of the dead.

Where priests had monopolized the ministry of Christian healing, the monarchs did likewise. They would often hold long services where the monarch would lay hands on sick persons and pray. While it was initially an act meant to support the divine right of kings, God did in fact use it for healing, much as he did use "last rites" on occasion to restore the sick to fullness of health, but such pigeonholing restricts the work of miracles and declares the gifts of lay persons as either inconsequential or lacking. Nothing could be farther from the truth.

The twentieth century saw the revival of Christian healing. It began in earnest in Los Angeles at the Azusa Street Revival. What made this a fresh expression of the spirit is that those who attended and were healed were from all walks of life—black and white, rich and poor, among those who kept the holiness code as well as hardened alcoholics, philanderers, and prostitutes. God was beginning to pour out his spirit upon all flesh. The recovered healing ministry in the Episcopal church essentially began in 1959 with the work of the Reverend Canon Dennis Bennett. Both Protestants and Catholics have charismatics.

How it Works

If a baptized person has discerned the gift of healing, do not discount it—work with it. Allow them to practice their prayer. Have them join in on the prayers you offer for the sick. Here is an outline I have found works for the ministry of healing:

- **Relax**—Get the sick person to relax and receive. Sitting is best.
- **Call down the Holy Spirit**: If you do not know how, you can use the hymn *Veni Creator Spiritus*, or *Veni Sancti Spiritus*, found in many hymnals.
- **Assess**—What is the ailment, is it spiritual or physical in nature?
- **Diagnose**—This is the time to be especially open to words of knowledge.
- **Ask for permission**—After assessing what is wrong, you may lay hands on the sick person only after obtaining consent.
- **Lay on hands**—If they, for example, have a hurting shoulder, ask to lay hands on the shoulder (use due discretion and keep in mind issues of modesty and personal space).
- **Anoint with oil**—Typically, the forehead is the best place. Occasionally, oil may be applied to an effected area. If they are doing the work of healing others, anoint their hands.
- **"Dipstick"**—Ask your sick person to report if they feel anything: heat, cool, movement, relaxation, or peace. This is also a time to observe for expressions of peace or a sudden flush of emotions, sometimes even tears of joy.
- **Refocus**—If the "dipsticking" is not yielding results, pray in a different way. Remember, this exercise is never a failure. God

always heals when we ask him. Sometimes, he just uses our prayers in a slightly different way than we imagined.

- **Close**—When it seems the praying has reached its natural conclusion, thank God for the work He has done. DO NOT say things like "You are healed." But look to Jesus' example who said, "Go and show yourself . . ." Let the medical professionals make that call.

Exercise:

Poll your congregations as to which of them would be interested in being part of a healing ministry. Gather them together and use a training resource. Educate them on the history of healing. Allow them to pray for each others' ailments. Talk about the results.

After training your lay healers, commission them as part of the Sunday service. You may use the official liturgies of your tradition for commissioning, or else use the form for the Commitment to Christian Service in *Book of Common Prayer* (p. 420). You may wish to give each healing minister a personal oil stock for use in their ministry and as a token of their commission.

I have found that the best place for a healing ministry is around the font. In this way, a team of two healers can serve multiple people. Have some chairs available so the person receiving the prayer can rest and receive. While you may choose to offer this ministry at times other than the Sunday liturgy, I have found that it works well during the distribution of communion. Remember, have your healers receive communion first, so they can be immediately dispatched to the font.

Meet with your mentor. How is healing ministry working for you. How is it affecting your lay-persons. Do you need to do more education? "Dipstick" your healers. How is the ministry working for them?

For Further Reading:

DeArteaga, William. *Quenching the Spirit: Examining Centuries of Opposition to the Moving of the Holy Spirit.* Lake Mary, FL: Creation House, 1992.

Fichter, Joseph H. *Healing Ministries: Conversations on the Spiritual Dimensions of Health Care.* New York: Paulist, 1986.

Hansen, Alan. *Healing and the Local Church.* Atlanta: Acts 29 Ministries, 2010.

Howe, John W. *Anointed by the Spirit: A Study of the Ministry of Jesus and His Followers.* Lake Mary, FL: Creation House, 2012.

Lenten Lessons

ONE OF THE BEAUTIES of the Lenten season is that you will have increased participation from your laypersons. One of your duties will be to construct or apply an educational series for midweek education. It has been my experience that "canned" series that are simply purchased do not usually draw the interest of the laity as do Lenten series that are constructed with the priest's particular ministry setting in mind. I have seen some congregations completely disengage from the Lenten experience because of a canned program that did not fit well into every tradition's experience (case in point—*The Purpose Driven Life*).

Preliminary Exercise:

List the major concerns of your parish. Ask if there is any deficient part of their learning. For example, if the parish is affluent and disengaged, would a series constructed around the corporal works of mercy work? If your congregation is Old Testament illiterate, would it be good for them to have a crash course in Old Testament?

You may also expound on one of the following topics:

- Prayer and Fasting
- Stewardship
- Evangelism
- The Sacraments

You may also take a longer look into Christian disciplines, such as:

- *Lectio Divina*
- The Rosary
- The Stations of the Cross
- Journaling
- Iconography
- Spiritual Direction
- The 12 Steps
- God in Christian Fiction
- Poetry and Psalmody
- The Interface between the Exodus and the Gospels
- Costly Discipleship
- The Saints of the Church
- What is Liturgy?

Exercise:

Develop a six-week course. Your program should run no more than one hour, and if there is homework for the next session, it also should be no more than one hour. Plan your series around a meal, perhaps something like soup and bread. Develop a sign-up sheet so your parishioners can provide the food.

Mentor Time:

Reflect with your mentor about this experience. How did the series go? Was it well attended? What could make this better? Could this series be shared with others? Could it be a resource for the larger church?

For Further Reading:

Gale, Elizabeth. *Programs for Lent and Easter*. Valley Forge, PA: Judson, 1991.

Hearing Confessions: Counsel and Penance

IN MY TRADITION, THE understanding of penance and auricular confession has been "All may, some should, none must" going back to the earliest days of the English Reformation. Many protestant faiths have an option for private confession. Often, those who avail themselves of a confession do not realize the immense weight that their consciences are holding until they are relieved of the burden.

In this exercise, we will look at the power of confession as a curative force to the soul. A series of three confessions are given. Your mentor will be the penitent, and you will be the confessor. If a great distance separates you, consider doing this exercise either by Skype or in front of an empty chair with your mentor on speakerphone. These are the actual confessions of real persons. They have been altered to protect confidentiality.

Confession One: *Subject is a sixty-year-old female, married. She has not made a confession in thirty years.*

> "Since my last confession, I have been burdened with one major thing. About thirty years ago, my husband was traveling abroad a great deal. He had a Japanese business partner who, my husband claimed, really liked me. He was in the middle of a big deal and, well . . . my husband thought it would be good for the business if I slept with him. It only happened once, and I can't say I enjoyed it. I don't know if I cheated, since it was my husband's idea. So for this sin and all I cannot now remember . . ."

- What counsel would you give the penitent?

- How would you alleviate her conscience?
- What act of contrition would you give?

Confession Two: Subject is a forty-two-year-old male, divorced with small children. He has never made a confession before. He is a regular parishioner.

> "Well padre, my life is a mess. I think I need some help. I don't know what came over me, but about three weeks ago, I got my hand caught in the cookie jar. I was taking a hundred dollar bill out of the register, just to get some groceries. You know, I don't mean to make excuses, but my hours keep getting cut, and I have no savings to lean back on. The boss lady said that she would give me a second chance and then gave me $50 of her own money. She said I didn't even need to pay her back. I put back the money and thanked my boss. I've never taken anything else like that before. And then I thought about what a conviction would do to my family. Oh, and I kinda got a problem with looking at the ladies a little too hard. I mean, it's not like I watch porn or sleep around, I just like to watch them a little too much. For these sins, and for those I cannot now remember..."

- What counsel would you give the penitent?
- How would you alleviate his conscience?
- What act of contrition would you give?

Confession Three: Subject is a sixteen-year-old developmentally challenged girl.

> "Mom says I need to be in here—that all of us do naughty things. Well I am so sick of her. She is so mean. I saw how things get better for her when she takes her pills. I started taking some of them too. I don't know if this is naughty or not. I mean, yeah, I steal 'em. Mom doesn't know. I'm sorry for the stealing part, but I just want to know the good feeling she gets from those pills, yah know. Well, for these sins, and for those I cannot remember..."

Hearing Confessions: Counsel and Penance

- What counsel would you give the penitent?
- How would you alleviate her conscience?
- What act of contrition would you give?

Since this is a delicate issue with a minor and possible drug abuse, what are the legal implications? How can you get her help, but preserve the pastoral privilege?

Mentor Time:

Discuss with your mentor his or her most difficult confessions. How does he or she decompress afterward? How does he or she arrive at a fitting act of contrition?

For Further Reading:

Gatta, Julia, and Martin Smith. *Go in Peace: The Art of Hearing Confessions.* London: Canterbury, 2013.

The Ecumenical Curate

> "We must all hang together, or assuredly we shall all hang separately."
>
> —Benjamin Franklin

ONE OF THE MOST challenging issues facing mainline churches is the shortage of resources. In a small-town context, it makes little sense to have an Episcopal youth group, a Presbyterian one, a Methodist one, and so on, if there are only three to five kids in each group. Without a critical mass of people, the group usually flounders. In such situations, it might be helpful to join forces to have an ecumenical youth group. But the list does not have to stop there.

Many facets of community life can benefit from cooperation. See below for some ideas:

- A cooperative picnic
- Community Easter sunrise service
- Building a Habitat for Humanity home
- Ecumenical Bible study
- Ecumenical soup kitchen
- A liturgical event that galvanizes community (e.g., if the community is Scottish, then the Kirking of the Tartans; if the community is primarily Mexican, then a festival of the Virgin of Guadalupe. Look to the demographics of your respective community).

- An interfaith nursing home visitation program (or caroling at a nursing home during the holidays)
- An interfaith revival inviting clergy from the local churches

While this is by no means an exhaustive list of the options, it is a starting point. Be creative.

Exercise:

Design a community event that can incorporate other churches and traditions. Perhaps even reach out to a local Jewish or Muslim congregation. Choose activities that benefit the community and impact people.

Mentor Time:

- What cooperative ministry would work in your community? Describe its birth and formation.
- What efforts did you take to organize this event or cooperative ministry?
- After it is in place, is there anything that you would do differently?

For Further Reading:

Schaller, Lyle. *From Geography to Affinity. How Congregations Can Learn From One Another*. Nashville: Abingdon, 2003.

Emergence for the Establishment

THE LATE EPISCOPAL BISHOP Mark Dyer was quoted as saying, "About every 500 years, the church has a rummage sale." This is to say that about every 500 years, the church has to re-evaluate its relevance and adapt for a changing world. Consider the history (dating is approximate):

- 1000 BCE—King David purchases the threshing floor upon which Solomon builds the first temple. The nomadic tabernacle is replaced with a permanent structure.
- 6th century BCE—Return from the exile in Babylon. The Jews learned that their identity did not depend on a particular place. Messianic expectation is now a common theme.
- 28 CE—The Jesus Tradition: Without a canon of scripture, apart from the Old Testament, and without a clear church hierarchy, the authority of the church is found in the oral Jesus Tradition. It is structuralized by the Apostle Paul and through the actions of the Council of Jerusalem (49 CE). The foundations of the Jesus Tradition are interpreted to be a worldwide movement, not simply a reformist Jesus sect.
- 325–787 CE—The age of the Seven Ecumenical Councils: The councils determined the limits of orthodoxy, formulated a creed, examined the role of the Virgin Mary, and dealt with major challenges to unity presented by the Arians, Pelagians, and Nestorians. It affirmed conciliarism as the government of the church. The early Christian Fathers are a foundation for the tradition of the Church.

- 1054 CE—The Great Schism: Differing opinions as to issues such as the Filioque clause, liturgical practices, and the universal primacy of Rome (used in a period when the Papacy and Roman Curia would be the defining source of authority until the Reformation) led to the separation of eastern and western Christianity.

- 1517 CE—The Protestant Reformation: addressed the rise of the excesses and abuses of Papal Rome (issues that Rome itself would only settle in the Second Vatican Council). The church appealed to scripture as the only source of true ecclesiastical authority.

- Today—The decline of Christendom culture: The church is and has been fighting the issues of civil rights, the role of women and minorities in the church, questions of sexual ethics; none of these can be answered by the previous standard of authority—namely, *Sola scriptura.*

So as you can see, we are in a time of one such change. We need only to look at our modern history to see that such a movement is taking place. We are asking hard questions that Scripture has been unable to answer definitively, such as, "Is slavery morally wrong?" The movement known as Emergence really can be said to begin with the abolitionists.

To deal with the young persons of this generation is to actively deal with issues of Emergence. The major rifts in the Episcopal Church can all be viewed as issues of Emergence: The "LGBT" movement, women's ordination, racial segregation and integration, and women's suffrage. On these topics, Scripture can be seen by some as ambiguous. The old authority could not answer definitively the issues of the day in light of new perspectives.

Along with the challenge of authority comes the issue of worship. We are no longer bound to a locality. Beginning with the invention of the Model T average families had other options than attending the village church. We began to travel outside of the counties of our birth. We began to explore other options with this new mobile culture. That mobile culture would turn into a global culture. The church failed to really take notice until about 1964. The mainline churches began to diminish. Young people, now exposed to eastern religions in Vietnam and in college classrooms began to question the uniqueness of Christianity. The church needed to adapt.

One such adaptation was the "seeker church." It provided a means to easy church membership, required little of members, and prized itself on openness. Unfortunately, the movement had little staying power. It appealed to seekers only and did not actively disciple. Mainline denominations often picked up these persons as they sought to dig deeper in their spiritual quest.

The Episcopal Church realized in the late 1960s that the strategies of the past were failing. It used to suffice to hang out a sign that said, "The Episcopal Church Welcomes You" and hold regular services, and people would join. However, the Field of Dreams philosophy, "If you build it, they will come," no longer works. The evolving American culture looked with suspicion at an institution that still worshiped with medieval liturgies and often *appeared* homophobic, misogynist, or racist. In the last twenty years, the college-aged generation continued to see the "Made in Europe" churches as museums of irrelevance.

What then are we to do? The following are trends that appear to have some power in retaining a new population of Christians:

- **Experiential worship**—A move away from predominantly auditory worship toward visual, kinetic, and tactile worship. Emergent worship includes the arts and often has multiple things going on at one time, much in the same way that Eastern Orthodox worship worships in Kairos time.

- **Unconditional positive regard**—This phrase, coined by psychologist Carl Rogers, approaches the Emergent idea of how to relate to others who are different from us. We reserve moralistic judgments and focus on the concept that each person is created in the image and likeness of God, regardless of race, ethnicity, lifestyle, age, or social class.

- **Midweek worship**—Gone are the days when the community comes together chiefly on Sundays. Now a thrust is being made to incorporate midweek worship in a post-Sunday culture. Average Sunday attendance is not a good measure of health in a world that no longer has blue laws and where young retail workers simply must work on Sunday.

- **Art, story, and play**—Emergent Christians tend to worship less in a didactic atmosphere and more in an experiential one. Visual art (including liturgical dance, painting, and pottery) is common. Moral problems and situations from Scripture may be acted out in play-like fashion instead of being verbally described by a preacher.

- **Eclectic form**—Borrowing from many different traditions and utilizing iconography, lights, meditation, yoga, soaking prayer, various languages, and differing styles of music, Emergent worship is a tapestry, not a strict and pure form. Worship should be fun, engaging, and fit the community, instead of making the community fit the form.

- **Neo-traditional**—Using elements from ancient Christian liturgies (Catholic and Orthodox). Anglican emergence often uses elements from Rite One liturgies.

Exercise:

Gather a few parishioners and experiment with some more adventurous types of worship. Perhaps use some different forms from old prayer books, invite parishioners to create and worship in their hearts. Remember, it is not your job to orchestrate it, rather to facilitate worship. Use elements that stimulate all five senses.

Questions:

- Did you use music? Recorded, live? How was it received?
- How did you use story?

- How were visual arts utilized?
- How did parishioners feel about this worship when they left?
- What would you do differently?
- Could you see this becoming a bigger part of your community?
- Would you like to offer this regularly? Why or why not?
- What about Emergence and emergent worship challenges you?

For Further Reading or Viewing

Gagne, Ronald. *Introducing Dance in Christian Worship*. Portland, OR: Pastoral, 1988.

Tickle, Phyllis. *Emergence Christianity—What It Is, Where It Is Going, and Why It Matters.* Dartmouth, MA: Baker, 2012.

Tickle, Phyllis, and Tim Scorer. *Embracing Emergence Christianity: A 6-Session Study*. New York: Church Publishing, 2011. (DVD)

Spiritual Direction

SPIRITUAL DIRECTION IS HELP given by one Christian (usually clergy) to another person (the directee) that assists the directee to understand God's way of communication, responding to God, growing in intimacy with God, and learning to better live according to the covenant established in baptism. Spiritual direction focuses on personal faith experience. It is concerned with relationship with God, not outward piety.

- **Spiritual direction is about a relationship**. The relationship finds its foremost setting in a life of prayer to which all other disciplines point.
- **Spiritual direction is a relationship that is progressing**. The task of the director is to facilitate the relationship progressing so that the relationship with God is getting stronger daily.
- **The real spiritual director is God**. God touches the human heart directly. The human spiritual director does not "direct" in the sense of psychotherapy (although that sometimes is needed as well). Rather, as director, he helps the directee respond to God's quest for us to know him as he is.

Spiritual direction can best be described as an art and not a science. In order to understand spiritual direction, we must first take a very close look at ascetical theology. What does it mean to say that you will practice your Christianity? Spiritual direction is all about understanding the ascetical nature of our spiritual lives and allowing someone to step into our very private prayer life and assist us on the road to becoming closer to God.

Perhaps you have never had a spiritual director. Perhaps it is an old discipline for you. Many times, as part of the pastoral privilege of being a rector or vicar of a congregation, you will be invited into very private parts of a person's spiritual journey. When this becomes a regular part of a pastoral relationship, you become a spiritual director.

It is unfair and unwise to ever serve as a spiritual director unless you yourself are also receiving spiritual direction. If you have spiritual directees, I suggest you have no more than two. I have found that it can be incredibly personally draining to be so intimately involved in a person's prayer journey, so be prepared for that.

The following are steps that may assist you with a spiritual direction meeting:

- **Establishing a baseline:** Ask your directee to do some homework before your first meeting. Ask them to list the major events in their life. What things made them feel close to God. What things made them feel as though God was far away? Ask if they have any struggles. Do they find it hard to pray? Do they find themselves in sin patterns? (Confession can be helpful here.) Ask them to write down their thoughts.

- **Have your initial meeting.** In the midst of the session, listen openly and earnestly. Always remember that this meeting is under the seal of pastoral confidentiality, so confidentiality is morally absolute for the director. Do you notice patterns? As you listen to the voice of the Holy Spirit, do you hear a plan of action?

- **Develop an ascetical plan.** What practices could be beneficial to your directee?

Look through the following list and trust your prayerful intuition to guide you. Remember—this is an art, not a science.

- Iconography
- Psychotherapy (by a professional, not the director!)

Spiritual Direction

- Guided meditation
- Prayerful painting or needlework
- *Lectio Divina*
- Cooking as a means to prayer
- Prayer using a musical instrument
- Taize
- Fasting
- Ruminating on a biblical mantra
- Confession
- Reading spiritual works (fiction and non-fiction)
- Inner healing
- Evangelism as a discipline
- The Rosary
- The breath prayer
- Gardening
- Service to others

This is by no means an exhaustive list, God may use these things to help you direct others or give you your own "bag of tricks."

Exercise:

- If you have not already found a spiritual director, search for one.
- What strategies does the director employ?
- How does it feel?
- Do you feel your relationship with God progressing?
- Are you closer to God?
- Have there been any surprises?

Optional Exercise:

Not everyone who happens to be a priest is a gifted spiritual director. If you choose to explore being a spiritual director, journal about the experience, being sure to leave out any information that might be of a confidential nature. You cannot share what you do not have yourself, so remember the best spiritual directors are in spiritual direction themselves.

Further Reading

Harton, F. P. *The Elements of the Spiritual Life*. Eugene, OR: Wipf & Stock, 2009.
Ignatius, of Loyola, Saint. *The Spiritual Exercises of St. Ignatius Loyola*. Baltimore, MD: Ignatius, 2010.
Thornton, Martin. *Spiritual Direction*. Cambridge, MA: Cowley, 1984.

Newcomer Assimilation

THE VAST MAJORITY OF churches would characterize their congregations as "friendly." However, it is often the case that many newcomers feel like outsiders—for good reason. The welcoming congregations are actually welcoming toward their own. Not surprising, these same congregations typically do not have a program to tend the front doors of their church. This requires an intentional plan to both assimilate newcomers and catechize them with the tenets of the faith.

Most churches have a simple plan to welcome new people. Perhaps they are given a grab bag with literature, perhaps a coffee cup and some candy or baked goods. In other churches, a representative from the congregation delivers a warm fresh loaf of bread to their home later that day. Both approaches have drawbacks. I have heard two responses: One stated that they felt that those measures were wonderful acts of caring (she had already decided to come back.) Some others say they feel that they are being "stalked" by being asked to stand and introduce themselves when they got their grab bag. Even worse, a person dropping by unannounced to deliver bread can have the appearance of stalking. It is important to recognize that most people decide whether to attend your church based on their first fifteen minutes of experiencing your church.

If you choose to use the grab bag approach, have greeters give them in private. There is no need to sound a trumpet before people who are probably thinking they will be trying other churches before settling on one. In this post-denominational age, most people under fifty will be trying many options in other denominations. Just because you might be the only church of your denomination in town does not mean you will have the advantage.

Curacy Express

After the initial contact, you will need to have some serious follow up. You will need to nurture a relationship with these newcomers. I suggest that you gather a group of gregarious parishioners who like speaking with new people and then implement a serious SERIES of contacts. It may help to compose a book, which notes the progression of newcomers from visitors to committed disciples. A spreadsheet for such a thing might look like this:

Visitor	Address Phone	First Visit to Parish	Follow up by Pastor	Greeting Committee	Small group	pledge card, regular
M/M John Doe (late fifties, empty nesters, new to town)	1414 Marcus St. 556-7224	5/21 Pentecost Sunday Follow-up letter mailed 5/24	Pastor called and offered visit 5/25	GC called and explained small groups 6/1	Couple attended Foyer group dinner 6/27	11/20 Consecration Sun. She is on Altar Guild He is investigating
Miss Mary Jones (Will be in town for college, family is Episcopalian)	321 College Road, Apt 5 227-2288	5/27 Trinity Sunday Follow-up letter mailed 5/29	Curate called and offered visit 5/28	GC called and explained church singles group	Attended Singles group 6/30	Parishioner asked for envelopes 7/15, prefers not to pledge until grants come in.

Newcomer Assimilation

If you put little into your newcomer assimilation, it will probably yield little. Newcomers need contact, opportunities and need to know that they are valued. If there is no follow up, chances are that you will not maximize the attractiveness of your parish.

For Further Reading:

www.shipoffools.com (a website dedicated to church visitation and the experiences of "mystery worshippers")

Michell, Neal. *How to Hit the Ground Running: A Quick-Start Guide for Congregations with New Leadership*. New York: Church Publishing, 2005.

The Catechumenate

During the last twenty years, the mega church movement has made church membership increasingly easy. People are less and less committed when they have to invest less of themselves. In this unit, we will be addressing the one feature of church membership that is guaranteed to build a church in faith AND numbers. Without a systematic plan of catechesis, your parish will gravitate toward a membership that is less and less committed and unable to explain their faith.

The early church had a dual reason for intense catechesis. For one, it needed to spread the fledgling church to every pocket of the world (a task we still have but rarely recognize the urgency). Secondly, since Christianity was illegal, it became a matter of security that spies who would act as informants for the Roman government would need to be identified. The original model, calling for a membership process lasting for three full years, is not practical today. However, a thorough approach to teaching the faith is essential.

The writings of St. Ambrose are replete with descriptions of how adults were formed in a program we know as the catechumenate. From these writings, the descriptions compiled by historians, and evidence found in the catacombs, we know what the early form of catechesis of adults looked like. Your task in this module is to design and implement the catechumenate to serve all those non-Episcopalians wishing to join your parish.

Step one: "What do you seek?" That question was asked of each person who was seeking baptism in the early church. The answer was "Life in Christ." You will begin a process which will be tailored to each group. The catechumenate should begin meeting whenever a candidate expresses a desire for baptism or to transfer from another denomination by confirmation, reaffirmation or reception. I recommend that you meet for no longer than an hour, and no more than twice per month. Peruse the materials placed at the end of this module for ideas, and take your cue from your catechumens. Each group will be different. A sample outline of topics might look like this:

November

Session One: "What Do You Seek?"—Looking into What Church Membership Means.

- Commitment
- Stewardship
- Initiation is only the beginning

Session Two: "Scripture, Tradition, and Reason"—Looking at the Authority of the Church.

- Historical look at the beginnings of Anglicanism
- The post-modern church—what has changed and what cannot change

December

Session One: "The Church Calendar"—Why Is Cosmology Important?

- The rhythm of the church year
- Understanding the seasons of the church, their meanings, colors, and symbols

Session Two: "The Life of Christ"—Looking at the Gospels

- Matthew—the gospel for the Jewish people
- Mark: the earliest gospel; "Messianic Secret"
- Luke: the gospel for the gentiles; women in the life of Jesus

- John: the gospel in macrocosm; I AM statements

January

Session One: "The Spiritual Life"—What Does It Mean to Practice Our Faith?

- Look at those who practice faith; bring lay leaders in to give testimonies
- Look at monastic life; Rule of St. Benedict; rules of life

Session Two: "What Is Liturgy?"—Taking a Close Look at What We Do in Church.

- Field trip into the church—take candidates to see sanctuary; look, touch, and feel.
- Tour the sacristy—what are the vessels and vestments used in services?

February

Session One: The History of Liturgy

- Old liturgies that older congregants remember well
- Talk about the development of liturgy as it relates to archeology and historical discoveries.

Session Two: Crash Course in Scripture

- The Old Testament—Law, Prophets, and History
- The Psalms—why are they so prominent in our liturgy?
- The Epistles—the church formulates its doctrine.
- Eschatology—Daniel and Revelation
- "The Word of God"—explore biblical inspiration, infallibility, inerrancy, literalism, fundamentalism, biblical criticism, quest for the historical Jesus.

The Catechumenate

March

Session One: Looking to Easter
- Talk about Lenten initiation rites found in historic liturgies.
- Begin plans for initiation.

Session Two: Lent—Why Is This Preparation Time So Special?
- Lenten disciplines—giving up and taking on
- What are self-denial, fasting, and almsgiving?

April

Session One: Mystagogy—The Neophyte Embraces His or Her Ministry
- Talk about the ministries offered in the church.
- Talk about ministries in the world (your ministry is where your joy and your gifts intersect).

Session Two: Feast Day
- Have a dinner together to celebrate the end of your catechumenate and the journey you shared together.

You may also have confirmation, reaffirmation, and reception at the same time as the baptisms. (This is ideal, but rarely happens except in cathedrals.) You might consider using a form of Christian commitment for those who are baptized, are completing the catechumenate, and will be confirmed, reaffirmed or received later, if your tradition has those resources

It is very important to have fun with catechesis. A lecture format will simply not work. Your candidates will need time to process and talk over issues of faith with you and fellow catechumens. This is an inductive exercise so let it have some latitude and let the process conform to the needs of that particular class of catechumens. Every year will be different.

Questions for Reflection:

- How did the group interact? Was there a dominant group?
- Were there more than one leaving a different faith background for Anglicanism? What was that like? Were you able to use their prior experiences to help them embrace the lessons?
- What was your experience with the rites of initiation? How did the candidates feel?
- What types of ministries were picked in the period of mystagogy? Were they predictable? Did the catechumenate influence their choice of ministry?

Mentor Time:

Discuss with your mentor their previous attempts at catechesis. What programs worked well? What programs failed? Discuss youth catechesis. Can parts of the catechumenal model serve to strengthen adolescent confirmation preparation? Would it help keep kids in church?

For Further Reading:

Cocoran, Bill. *Preparing the Rites of Initiation*. Collegeville, MN: Liturgical, 1997.

Harmless, William, SJ. *Augustine and the Catechumenate*. Collegeville, MN: Liturgical, 1995.

Libby, Bob. *Coming to Faith*. Lincoln, NE: Author's Choice, 2002.

Packer, J. I., and Gary A. Parrett. *Grounded in the Gospel: Building Believers the Old Fashioned Way*. Grand Rapids, MI: Baker, 2010.

Lucado, Max, and Randy Frazee. *The Story: The Bible as One Continuing Story of God and His People*. Grand Rapids, MI: Zondervan, 2011. (A valuable book to help new Christians fall in love with Scripture without being overwhelmed)

Constructing a Sermon Series

In most cases, mainline protestant Christians are not accustomed to a sermon series. Most homilists preach specifically on the gospel, lesson proper, or else one of the lessons. Unfortunately, the vast majority of people understand the Scriptures in a series of stories without understanding their relationship to one another and to the journey of God's faithful people throughout all of salvation history. Our liturgical heritage is, however, a treasury. One of the basic gifts that makes a sermon series possible is the gift of the lectionary.

The new Revised Common Lectionary has peculiar genius in its arrangement of a thematic-based structure. It groups into two tracks Old Testament lessons that, when paired with a psalm, provide a perfect place to explore the Old Testament in progression. During ordinary time, it would be possible to do at least six sermon series in as many years, simply by opting to preach from the Old Testament.

The epistles also follow sequentially, beginning with Romans in year A. If you are a preacher that enjoys preaching the doctrinal foundation of the church, stick with the epistle lesson. Such sermons can be wonderfully foundational when, for example, you look at the common life of the church in the Book of Acts during Eastertide. Sermon series can be helpful during Lent if the subject matter or lessons can be tied into a theme for your Lenten series. Likewise, Advent offers such opportunities for preparation.

Exercise:

Select three weeks where either the Old Testament or Epistle runs sequentially (it is best to do this in the seasons after Pentecost and Epiphany at first). Pick out thematic elements in the lessons and give a sermon series. You can base it on an exegetical approach to the Scriptures appointed or a thematic overview that touches on twenty-first century issues. Have fun. Advertise that this is what you are doing and try to build some momentum. Some people may just make their regular attendance happen because they want the next segment in the story.

Follow up:

Ask three of your most trusted and honest parishioners, "What did you like or not like about the series?" Take their considerations into account the next time you choose to preach a series.

If you were able to incorporate your series into a season (an example would be looking at the seven deadly sins during Lent), did the series add to the theme of the season? Did it dovetail with other events, studies, or classes offered at the same time?

For Further Reading:

Berkley, James, ed. *Preaching to Convince*. Waco, TX: Word, 1985.
Craddock, Fred B. *Preaching*. Nashville: Abingdon, 1985.
Crum, Milton. *Manual on Preaching*. Valley Forge, PA: Judson, 1977.

Using Your Lay Persons to Their Fullest

THE LEVEL OF COMMITMENT of the average church member is less than stellar. It is noted that in this very mobile culture, most lay persons who frequent our pews tend to do so only once a month—and that is considered good attendance these days! In this module, we will examine some simple techniques that will help you build a fire of commitment in your parishioners.

Please note, if you do not do step one through three, you can forget four and five.

Step one: Make an effort to strike up regular conversations. Keep a notebook of the passions or interests of your members. Make sure they know you love them.

Step two: Practice active listening. When in conversation, listen intently. Clarify any miscommunications.

Step three: Visit your parishioners. Remember the tribal nature of congregations. You need to develop relationships, or your parishioners will not be committed. Moreover, if you show that you are willing to invest in them, they will be willing to invest in your ministry.

Step four: Identify passions. If a parishioner has recently gotten married, this is the time to talk about a young couples' group. If a parishioner has an incarcerated brother and that seems to occupy the discussions, it may be time to look at Kairos ministry.

Step Five: Birth a Ministry. When trust has been solidified and it is obvious that your lay person respects and values your leadership, it is time to birth the ministry. Create a meeting time when you can affirm the relationship, give homage to the passion of your soon-to-be new leader and then suggest the new endeavor. Be prepared for a bit of questioning or even resistance. Encourage them to know God is affirming the call through the clergy and you will be there along the way to help, guide, and direct where needed.

"Eagles' Wings"

> *Eagles are incredible parents. They insist that the eaglets learn autonomy. By the time that the mother eagle determines that the eaglet is able to fly, she begins pushing her young one out of the nest. As the eaglet is pushed out of the tree and begins to fall, the father eagle flies below and catches the eaglet on his wings. This scenario is repeated until the eaglet gets the hang of flying on his own. In Isaiah 40, God is likened to such a father eagle, raising us up on eagles' wings lest we dash our foot against a stone. You too, as a clergy leader will be there to raise up your little eaglets until they can fly on their own. That is leadership. That is pastoring. You must push you eaglets out of the nest or you will be feeding them with infant food forever. But never push the new minister out without being their safety net.*

Step Six: Refresh your relationships. Don't forget the birthday cards, thank you notes, and occasional letters (or emails) of encouragement to your ministry heads. Building a parish and crystalizing lay involvement must include efforts that demonstrate that their ministry is important to you.

Step Seven: Give them space: It is wonderful for clergy to be involved in lay ministry. It is quite another when the direction is so precise it borders on micromanagement. Give your people space to approach you when needed, but allow them the freedom to practice their ministry.

It seems laborious, but this process must be done with every lay leader individually. The business of cultivating relationships takes time. Be patient. General Motors did not add all of its car lines on its first day of production

Exercise

Find a person who has been on the fringes of your congregation. Make it a point to make a house call. Practice steps one through four. Cultivate a relationship and as their attendance becomes more regular, move into steps 5–7. Report on the growth of the relationship with your mentor.

For Further Reading/Viewing:

Dent, Barbara. *The Gifts of Lay Ministry.* Notre Dame, IN: Ave Maria, 1989.
Hansen, Alan. *Why Is Moving From Churchgoer to Disciple So Important?* Atlanta, GA: Acts 29 Ministries, 2009. (DVD)

Building the Guiding Coalition

NO PRESIDENT HAS EVER governed without a cabinet. No wise CEO would ever change a corporate game plan without the endorsement of his board of directors. Likewise, no pastor should endeavor to lead any change without a guiding coalition. While never found in the official titles of official church-speak, a leader cannot expect to successfully lead planned change until the tribal structure of the church has signed on to the process.

First, what is a guiding coalition and what is it not? A guiding coalition is an advisory panel that meets with the rector. Suitable persons on the guiding coalition would be the parish matriarch or patriarch, storyteller, or the heads of large families with multiple generations attending your parish. It is an appointed group and it reports to no one except the rector. A guiding coalition is not normally the board. The guiding coalition is not the pastor's friends. It is not elected or changing. It is not a place where newcomers belong. The purpose of a guiding coalition is for the pastor to win over the "old guard" with new and fresh ideas, receive consent from the "old guard" to implement them and to garner the wisdom of history which probably goes back well beyond the rector's tenure. Without a guiding coalition, you risk stepping in a mess that is not easy to clean up and may very well cost you your ministry.

Looking at your current congregation

- Which members represent the old guard?
- Who has automatic veto power of any new initiative?
- Who has the longest tenure of membership?

Building the Guiding Coalition

- Who do the people turn to when you are unavailable?

If you answer these questions, you will know who needs to be on your guiding coalition.

How often should the guiding coalition meet?

The size and style of your congregation dictate the need for meetings. The larger the congregation and the more ministry initiatives it has will dictate more frequent meeting. Most congregations that are pastoral, transitional, or program-sized need a monthly meeting. Family-sized churches might do well with a quarterly meeting.

Exercise:

Assemble five persons to serve on your guiding coalition. Explain to them the need and that you value their commitment and collective wisdom. When choosing the members, you may opt to ask the office staff and vestry who really has the unseen clout in the parish. Plan your meeting, talk over your new plans **before implementing them**, and report to your mentor. Here are some questions for thought:

- How did the group interact?
- Was there any opposition to new ministry plans?
- What was the feel of the room? Did they show any hostility, gratitude, or excitement?
- Did the guiding coalition endorse your ideas? Refine them?
- What made you glad you consulted them?

For Further Reading:

Myra, Harold. *Leaders: Learning Leadership from Some of Christianity's Best.* Waco, TX: Word, 1985.

Martyrs, Manipulators, and Mayhem

Dealing with the Problematic Parishioner

EVERY CONGREGATION IS THE body of Christ, and every congregation also figures into the larger body of Christ. Just as we are many members with Jesus at the head, occasionally churches, like the body, will be subject to infection and even, occasionally, cancer. In this module we will look at what the biblical understanding is of church functions, and what is a biblical response when one member goes rogue.

- The phrase "the body of Christ" is a common New Testament metaphor for the church (the invisible unity of the baptized). The church is called "one body in Christ" in Romans 12:5, "one body" in 1 Corinthians 10:17, "the body of Christ" in 1 Corinthians 12:27 and Ephesians 4:12, and "the body" in Hebrews 13:3. The church is analogized as "the body" of Christ in Ephesians 5:23 and Colossians 1:24.

- Members of the body of Christ are joined to Christ in salvation (Ephesians 4:15–16).

- Members of the body of Christ follow Christ as their head (Ephesians 1:22–23).

- Members of the body of Christ are the physical representation of Christ in this world. The church is the organism through which Christ manifests his life to the world today.

- Members of the body of Christ are indwelt by the Holy Spirit of Christ (Romans 8:9).

- Members of the body of Christ possess a diversity of gifts suited to particular functions (1 Corinthians 12:4-31). "The body is a unit, though it is made up of many parts; and though all its parts are many, they form one body. So it is with Christ" (verse 12).
- Members of the body of Christ share a common bond with all other Christians, regardless of background, race, or ministry. "There should be no division in the body, but . . . its parts should have equal concern for each other" (1 Corinthians 12:25).
- Members of the body of Christ are secure in their salvation (John 10:28-30). For a Christian to lose his salvation, God would have to perform an "amputation" on the body of Christ!
- Members of the body of Christ partake of Christ's death and resurrection (Colossians 2:12).
- Members of the body of Christ share Christ's inheritance (Romans 8:17).
- Members of the body of Christ receive the gift of Christ's righteousness (Romans 5:17).

So, if the body is well functioning, its constituents complement each other instead of fighting one another. Unfortunately, the church of the New Testament and the church of today are no different. We have quarrels, and that disrupts the good functioning of the church. The church in Corinth had a particular issue with civil litigation in the church. The recipe for addressing such problems can be found in Matthew's gospel:

> If your brother sins against you, go and tell him his fault, between you and him alone. If he listens to you, you have gained your brother. But if he does not listen, take one or two others along with you, that every charge may be established by the evidence of two or three witnesses. If he refuses to listen to them, tell it to the church. And if he

refuses to listen even to the church, let him be to you as a Gentile and tax collector. (18:15–17 NRSV)

How much easier it would be if all of our churches would follow the Lord's own advice concerning such disputes! If a problematic parishioner is causing dissention in the church, recognize that such dissention is, in fact, sin. Often agendas are not viewed as sinful by our parishioners or, heaven forefend, even our leaders. We have but one agenda and that is the Lord's, and any deviation from unity among the baptized is sin. Furthermore, if left to rot, such a divisive sin may become schism.

Step 1: An individual visit is warranted. It is not the time during coffee hour, a vestry meeting, or function. A priest would do well to consider making a home visit. If there is still dissention, see if there can be an understanding. Remember that you are acting as an agent of healing. Your job is not to win an argument, but to persuade a toxic person to be healed and thereby reconcile the congregation with her members.

Step 2: If the parishioner is still causing havoc, ask a few of your guiding coalition members to accompany you. Give them a full account of what has transpired and let them know that your aim is healing and reconciliation. If the problematic parishioner repents, wonderful; if not, proceed to step 3.

Step 3. Having completed steps one and two, if the problematic parishioner is still not responding, it is time for a letter to the church. It is not wise to engage this issue from the pulpit, so written correspondence is best. If the parishioner does not repent, issue a decree of excommunication, carbon copy the bishop, and state your case in written form.

It has been my experience that rarely will it process beyond step one. The person will either repent or take his or her presence elsewhere.

Problematic parishioners take many forms, and such sociodynamics are important for parish priests to understand. You may wish to re-acquaint yourself with the unit on family systems. No manipulator ever exists without a martyr to sustain him or her. Remember to be a non-anxious change agent.

Nota Bene

There is no exercise for this unit because conflict comes when we least expect it. If you have some form of conflict and use any of the above tools, be sure to have a conversation with your mentor.

Stewardship Success

Designing a Stewardship Program from the Ground Up

STEWARDSHIP IS A FUNNY word, and it is grossly misunderstood in most churches. Typically, a stewardship drive is launched in order to meet the budget needs of the church. A vestry or finance committee meets and estimates what the expenses of the coming year will be, and an attempt is made to find the necessary pledges to fit such a need. Some churches even ponder a "faith budget" which prayerfully hopes for the discrepancy between income and expense to be met by God's intervention. In any case, this is fundraising, not stewardship, and in this module, we shall revisit what it is to be a good steward and work together to provide a stewardship program.

Stewardship is a year-round issue. Jesus spent a large portion of his time preaching about priorities, including finances. But before you think about stewardship as a money thing, let us look at what it is biblically: the disposition of the whole person toward the objectives and goals of the kingdom of God.

Secondly, stewardship is not about tithing, although it is a part of it. While the biblical standard of the tithe is indeed the minimum standard of Christian giving, stewardship encompasses so much more. For the purposes of this module, we will not look at stewardship in response to a church's needs, but rather the needs of the one practicing stewardship well.

Let us look at the *whole person*. God desires that we be totally and completely his. The great problem is that many of us live compartmentalized lives. We may invite God into our families, but not our finances. God may be welcome in our church attendance, or outreach, but absent from our sexuality. The following is a list of common issues and places in our lives. Stewardship programs should address all of them:

Church attendance—Stewardship should raise the issue of how often we attend worship and how dedicated we are to making that a priority.

Volunteerism—Do we use our time to better the kingdom of God on earth by helping people without financial remuneration?

Financial giving—Do we give to the causes supporting the kingdom of God in like measure as we have been blessed? Please note, the tithe is helpful here, but it must be noted that God honors those who are attempting to get their budgets in line and tithe at a predetermined future date. Do we give lovingly, or half-heartedly, or out of obligation?

Family time—Do we reserve enough time for family members, carving out special time for each?

Spouse—Do husbands love their wives as Christ loved the church, so much that they would lay down their life for them? Do wives support their husbands and encourage them to be men of God and people of character.

Sexuality—Often in our post-Victorian culture, we talk about sexuality either with shame, disgust, or lurid perversity. Do we use our sexuality to glorify God by reserving it for our spouse only, single persons abstaining from sex altogether, and resisting the temptations of pornography and suggestive novels or explicit television programs?

Disposable income—Is the amount of money we reserve for fun used in a godly manner, or in pursuit of hedonism?

Personal ministries—Are we living into the call that God is giving for each member of the body of the baptized, or are we running, resisting, or otherwise opposing God's will for our ministry?

Attitude—Are we ruled by strife and anger, or are we attempting to be on good terms with others and be a community (and therefore individuals) ruled by the law of love?

Personal hygiene—Do we care for the body as God's own creation, loving it as God loves us, therefore using food and substances with a spirit of temperance and self-control?

Environmental care—Do we take time to realize the effects of our purchases and behaviors—how they affect the world we will one day leave? Do we show concern for our children by giving them a better, cleaner world?

Others—Do we love others in the power of the Spirit and work toward banishing all attitudes that we are somehow better than others? Do we confront our own biases and prejudices knowing that others may hold things against our particular classification?

Having examined the above-mentioned facets, we see that the typical stewardship design offered in most parishes is woefully lacking. God wants all of us, and ***all of*** all of us. We owe it to our parishioners to help them embrace true stewardship and help them grow.

Exercise

Design a stewardship program that focuses on total stewardship, not simply meeting a budgeted need. Make this a yearlong effort. Share ideas with your mentor. Test and see if parishioners will be more giving financially when the church is interested in their total stewardship. Run the idea over with your mentor. Ask him or her what has worked for them in the past.

For Further Reading/Viewing:

Ball, Arthur. *Let Us Give*. Grand Rapids, MI: Kregel, 2003.
Hansen, Alan W. *Stewardship and Financial Growth*. Atlanta, GA: Acts 29 Ministries, 2009. (DVD)
Phillippe, William R. *A Stewardship Scrapbook*. Louisville, KY: Geneva, 1999.

The Demanding Lover

When Faithful Ministry Becomes an Obstacle to Marriage

IN A PREVIOUS UNIT, we looked at the perils of a poorly planned workweek. This unit looks at the stewardship of family time. My wife often reminds me that the vows I took to her long preceded my ordination vows. It seems to be the curse specifically of hardworking, possibly overfunctioning leaders that they so love their work that it becomes stressful on their marriages. Many a good marriage has been ruined by the demanding mistress of ministry.

A Case Story

Virginia was a very capable leader and priest. She had served two churches, one as a curate and then as a rector of a small, suburban town. Her church quickly became known as the only church in the area with a "lady priest." She did a very good job, stabilized finances, started a new church school, and brought her ASA up by 35 people to 105. She loved her job and her people loved her. All the while her very devoted husband became resentful. She was spending more and more time in the field or in the office. Sam, her husband, became a victim of a very insidious problem—when good ministry is so consuming that it becomes a type of adultery.

They entered therapy. Sam was willing to work on the relationship, but Virginia just didn't get it. The ministry had become a sort of drug to her. She needed being needed. Unfortunately, she did not realize that her husband needed her more than her parishioners. After a year and a half, the couple separated.

That story does not have to be common, but it is. At a funeral for a fellow priest, I heard a tear-streaked daughter say, almost with pride, "To my dad, the church always came first." While I understood that she meant that as a good thing, she missed out on having a deeper relationship with her father.

Let us be clear. Doing a good job is of paramount importance. A good spouse will also understand that Christmas, Easter, and Holy Week will be stressful times and will demand a lot of energy out of the cleric (and family). But when the ministry becomes "a lover," then it has become something that needs an overhaul.

Exercise:

Sit down with your wife or husband. Consider the following questions and rate them from one to ten. Use different colors of pens, perhaps red and blue. Rank how problematic these issues have been in your marriage. (Note: this is not an exercise in guilt or shame, but an opportunity to grow.)

1–Not at all

2–Very little

3–Somewhat

4–Becoming problematic

5–Definitely problematic

Clergy Questions:

My spouse has taken a backseat to my ministry.	1 2 3 4 5
My spouse typically is wondering when I will be able to come home.	1 2 3 4 5

I *appear* to crave time with my work more than with my spouse.   1 2 3 4 5

My family and friends say I put too many hours on the job.   1 2 3 4 5

My level of energy when I come home is often too little to have a meaningful relationship with my wife/husband or family.   1 2 3 4 5

I am so overworked that I have little time for romance, sex, or play.   1 2 3 4 5

I check my cell phone or email to make sure that I am not missing work-related information, even when on vacation or a family trip.   1 2 3 4 5

Spouse Questions:

I feel like I have taken a backseat to my spouse's ministry.   1 2 3 4 5

I often wonder when my spouse will be able to come home.   1 2 3 4 5

My spouse seems to crave time with work more than with me.   1 2 3 4 5

I feel my spouse puts too many hours on the job.   1 2 3 4 5

My spouse has little energy when he/she comes home, often too little to have a meaningful relationship with our family.   1 2 3 4 5

My spouse is so overworked that he/she has little time for romance, sex, or play.   1 2 3 4 5

The Demanding Lover

My spouse checks his/her cell phone or email to make sure that he/she is not missing work related information, even when on vacation or a family trip.   1 2 3 4 5

Total the corresponding numbers. Compare your scores and talk about any large differences in scoring. If your numbers are both high, you have identified an area needing work; you might want to consider some intentional scheduling changes, and, if necessary, some professional marriage counseling.

For Further Reading:

Merrill, Dean. *Clergy Couples in Crisis: The Impact of Stress on Pastoral Marriages.* Waco, TX: Word, 1985.

Coping with Crisis

As Local as Your Church and as National as 9/11

THE LIKELIHOOD OF HAVING a major catastrophe happen during your ministry is probably quite small. However, life is uncertain and clergy are called to serve at some of the most difficult times in life. Natural disasters, death, accidents, rape, assault, robbery, shootings, and domestic violence are a part of our lives. Unless we, as clergy, can be "salt and light" to a hurt and broken world, we are useless when those who depend on us for leadership and healing reach for their hands in need.

So what constitutes a crisis? Episcopal priest Robinson Dewey, a cleric who has devoted his life to crisis chaplaincy, states the following: "A crisis is a crisis to the person having the crisis." We cannot know what is going through the mind of a person, or ever have good enough words to say. What we have to offer is ourselves. When clergy can be emotionally present and look with the same empathy with which Jesus looked upon the harassed and helpless, then we will be doing our job.

As clergy, we may also be called into a situation where those to whom we minister may not be of the same faith as us. It is OK to take off the collar and get dirty. The following is a minor list of things to keep in mind when responding to a "critical incident."

- You can *never* understand, so do not claim to be able to do so.
- Never hug a rape victim, their personal space has been violated in the most extreme way.
- Do not act shocked at any of the events; you have a job to do.

- Feel free to cry, that makes you no more or less of a priest.
- Offer prayer when appropriate; if not welcome, pray in your head.
- Remember that your job is not to fix the problem, but to love through the problem.
- Keep a kit in your car that includes: oil stock, pyx (with five communion hosts), stole, antibacterial gel, band aids (in case YOU get cut), tissues, and a pocket Bible.)

Perhaps the most blessed advice I ever received in my ministry was from an FBI chaplain who had been a responder to the World Trade Center cleanup. In the mix of cloud and ash, with human remains scattered and the smell of death in the air, my friend realized: TO BE PRESENT *IS* FAITHFUL MINISTRY! We need not worry about what *we* are equipped to offer. God offered us his Son, and we are representatives of him. Sometimes being there is most of the battle. He will give us what we need when we need it.

Decompression and Self-Care

Crisis ministry is incredibly taxing. In the course of your life, God has already given you tools to deal with the stress of ministry in a positive and uplifting way. Here are some of the things you might use to decompress after a critical event:

- Needlework
- Listening to praise music
- Listening to chant
- Gardening
- Playing a musical instrument
- Painting
- Journaling
- Watching a comedy

- Spending time with pets
- Cooking/baking
- Board games
- Playing cards with family

Exercise:

Today we will do an exercise in role-play. If you are able to sit with your mentor, all the better. If not, then you can sit facing an empty chair with your mentor on speakerphone. Your task is to debrief a survivor.

Scenario:

Mary has seen her husband, John, acting erratically lately. He has been doing some totally bizarre things. He stored the dirty dinner dishes in the linen closet. His speech has been erratic. The children, a four-year-old girl and two-year-old boy, do not understand what has happened to their dad. John hasn't gone to work in a few days either. Mary hasn't mentioned any of this to anyone at church; she is embarrassed and does not understand his behavior. John has never been a user of drugs or alcohol, so it just doesn't make sense.

Fifteen minutes ago, your cell phone rang. The police department called and asked you to come for a visit. John hanged himself in the closet while Mary was at the grocery store. The children found his body. Mary is waiting, seated in the living room when you get there. Act out the scene with your mentor. Talk about the results. Compare experiences.

For Further Reading:

Berkley, James D. *Called into Crisis: The Nine Greatest Challenges of Pastoral Care.* Dallas, TX: Word, 1989.

Kubler-Ross, Elizabeth. *Working It Through.* New York: MacMillan, 1982.

Moving Out or Moving On

A Pastor Ponders a Change in Ministry Placement

A WISE BISHOP (NOW retired) once told me, all of us are *locum tenetes*, that is, temporary holders of the seat. Our ministries will have a beginning, a middle, and also most assuredly an end. We will examine in this module the choices surrounding seeking a new ministry assignment and, furthermore, the implications of such a move.

This may seem a bit premature; after all, this is your first assignment. In short order, you will be in another location. Some things will be constant. Your people will need to be loved, nurtured, and empowered. This will happen whether you are an assistant in an urban center or a curate-in-charge at a missionary outpost in the middle of the country. The aim of your judicatory—and of *Curacy Express*—should be to give you the tools to be successful at ministry and, hopefully, to help you fall in love with the unique ministry setting of the local church with a desire to stay and build the kingdom together. We pray that has been your experience.

Moving On, or Moving Up?

As noted earlier in the segment on congregational size, family-sized churches (which make up the bulk of middle America) are often plagued by rectors who come for a season. They come seeking a place to establish a name and then move on. These little churches never get a fighting chance, and it is reflected in their histories and attitudes.

Curacy Express

The job of *Curacy Express* is to help you fall in love with ministry and give you tools for success, whether the church has an ASA of five or five-hundred. We need missionary pastors, not those hoping to use smaller churches as a stepping-stone for the eventual aim of some large, affluent ministry.

Years ago, I had the wonderful benefit of being a transitional deacon, and then seven months later, priest-in-charge of my own congregation. It was a wonderful spot, just outside of Peoria, Illinois, in a small town called Morton. The bishop was thinking that it might need to be closed. Only twenty-three people worshipped there on an average Sunday. They had gone through five years of supply priests. There was no endowment, just some small stocks. They managed to scratch together enough for two years of full-time pay and a belief in the provision of God that somehow, this then twenty-nine-year-old might give them a future.

I made so many mistakes. There was no program like *Curacy Express* then, and it became my resolve that future priests would be able to learn from a text and mentorship instead of having to make hard mistakes themselves. By the grace of God, the average Sunday attendance for this small church rose from twenty-three to forty-five during my two years. I can credit only the unmerited favor of God, simply because, in retrospect, I had little clue what I was doing. At the end of the two years, I made the difficult decision to leave. I had to provide for my family and this church was not where God was moving me. The pain was intense. I had never loved such a group so much. As a final gesture, I invited them to consider a new way of life as a yoked congregation. Today, even though small, they are a proud small church with a big ministry impact, even though yoked with a neighboring parish.

My point is this: leaving a church is hard, emotional work. I grieved this well into my next ministry assignment. I think it is far better to invest yourself deeply than to fail to invest out of fear. God is the orchestrator, and only God knows the future of your ministry efforts.

Moving Out or Moving On

"Feast on the memories of the good times; they will be your manna when things are not so good."

—A former spiritual director of mine

The Effect of Long Tenure:

Most churches never get the opportunity to really grow. Statistics tell us that rectors who stay with churches for seven years are really only beginning to see the effect they will have. The most powerful years of growth are between seven and fourteen years. It would also be wise to add that at year seven, the pastor typically goes on a three-month sabbatical to gather a new vision, and in all fairness the returning rector should stay at least a year after the sabbatical. If you remember the tribal nature of the parish you will see a certain pattern:

- Year one—Excitement (feed on it, you will need the memories).
- Year two—The lull as the excitement wears off. Keep building relationships.
- Year three—New initiatives fade, time to be building relationships in earnest.
- Year four—First year of major growth. The vestry is now occupied by allies of the rector.
- Years five through seven—Stability and more relationships (and sabbatical time)
- Years seven through fourteen—Sustainable growth

Here are some questions to ask yourself when contemplating a ministry change. Please note that these are just to help you ask yourself the tough questions. It is NEVER easy. There will always be mixed emotions, perhaps even a trace of guilt. The whole process must be absolutely soaked in prayer, and your entire family needs to be on the same page.

- Do I feel my work here is done?

- Has God placed a particular new ministry on my heart?
- Is there a different parish that just keeps calling out to me?
- Is God closing doors and opening others?
- Are finances dictating that I MUST look for another position?
- Is my family thriving in this location or lingering on the vine?
- Will leaving now do damage to my current congregation, or would it be good for them too?
- Am I running out of ideas and has ministry become stale, rote or dull?
- Have I been encouraged by others to seek a new call?
- Has my wife or husband encouraged me to look for a new call?

Exercise:

Confer with your mentor about his or her ministry transitions. What has gone well and what could have been done better? Ask him or her the following questions:

- Did you ever stay in a church too long? If so, why?
- Did you ever leave too soon?
- What events led you to believe that God was calling you to a new ministry situation?
- Have you ever had a long tenure? What did that do for your ministry?
- If you could go back and correct anything you have done in the past at a former parish, what would it be?

For Further Reading:

Bickers, Dennis W. *The Tentmaking Pastor: The Joy of Bivocational Ministry.* Grand Rapids, MI: Baker, 2000.

Moore, Christopher C. *Opening the Clergy Parachute: Soft Landings for Church Leaders Who Are Seeking a Change.* Nashville: Abingdon, 1995.

Quotes from Seasoned Pastors:

"Don't try to be perfect—you will fail every time. The greatest lesson I have learned is that we need to accept our own shortcomings."

                        The Reverend Bernard T. Flynn

"Make sure your deacon isn't the matriarch of the parish."

                        The Reverend Glen DeShaw

"Many church members would rather see the church die than change."

                        The Very Reverend Dr. Kevin Martin

"Never assume that parishioners would not foster their own agenda."

                        The Reverend J. James Gerhart

"Nothing prepares you for the reality of dealing with the messy problems of people's lives. It's very humbling to be invited into their messes."

                        The Reverend Kay Wiggins

Curacy Express

"Apologize early. Apologize often. Apologize sincerely. You don't know as much as you think you do."

The Reverend Michael Bertrand

"No matter how long you are in a parish, you will always think you can get more done that you actually can—do not lose heart."

The Reverend Canon Dr. J. Douglas McGlynn

Review and Certification:

AT THIS POINT YOU have concluded a massive amount of training. Great trust has been placed in you by your bishop and the congregation(s) you have served. You have been formed further into the character of a pastor and, equally as important, a leader.

At this point, a review will be done by the judicatory concerning your progress in the program. If your judicatory leader deems that you have adequately learned from the program, you can receive a certificate of completion of *Curacy Express*. We trust that God will use you to bless his people in the wider church and to the glory of Almighty God. May God bless you in your ministry.

www.ingramcontent.com/pod-product-compliance
Lightning Source LLC
Chambersburg PA
CBHW071443160426
43195CB00013B/2019